TOO CLOSE TOO SOON

TOO CLOSE TOO SOON

DR. JIM A. TALLEY AND DR. BOBBIE REED

THOMAS NELSON PUBLISHERS®
Nashville

A Division of Thomas Nelson, Inc.
www.ThomasNelson.com

Published in Nashville, Tennessee, by Thomas Nelson, Inc.

Library of Congress Cataloging-in-Publication Data

Talley, Jim A.
Too close, too soon. Includes study guide
p. cm.
ISBN 07852-6474-4 AACR2
1. Single people—Sexual behavior—Religious aspects—Christianity.
2. Sexual ethics—Religious aspects—Christianity. I. Reed, Bobbie.
II. Title.
HQ800.T34
306.7'0880652 82-2132

Printed in the United States of America

04 05 06 PHX 5 4

To my wife, Joyce.
We learned many of the principles in this book through
our courtship and the years of marriage since 1961.
What little I know about the opposite sex
has taken that long to learn!
—JIM TALLEY

To Charles Edward Reed
with love and appreciation
for the nineteen happy years
of our marriage.
—BOBBIE REED

CONTENTS

INTRODUCTION

Today 47 percent of the American adult population is single. The tragedy of this statistic is that a majority of those who are single are *single again*. This is indicative of the divorce rate, which in some parts of our country has reached the 75-percent level!

The dissolution of a marriage signifies a relationship that failed, often because the two people involved were swept into marriage by "eromania" (romantic love) and never took the time to develop the skills required to make a relationship work. Falling in love with and being sexually attracted to a member of the opposite sex is no guarantee for a successful marriage. A marriage is more than romance and sex. It is an ongoing relationship that requires a lot of hard work.

Yet all too often, relationships (friendships, dating relationships, or marriages) do not survive the harsh realities of everyday life. Preferring the easy excitement of romance to the complexities of genuine relationships, many people seem to get involved in "revolving door alliances." They couple, go around together until they are bored, then exit the relationship.

People abandon relationships for various reasons: unrealistic expectations, diminishing excitement, excessive conflicts, poor relational skills, or lack of understanding between partners. Relationships between men and women are complicated interactions that take a significant amount of time and energy to develop. Those that progress too quickly through the various stages of intimacy are not strong enough to endure the inevitable confrontations over conflicting needs and desires. Yet in today's world of instant gratification, many people do not give relationships time to grow, to develop, and to prove that they are stable enough before marriage is proposed.

A recent secular study indicated that 85 percent of males and 75 percent of females become sexually active by age nineteen ("Teen Sex and Pregnancy," The Alan Guttmacher Institute, March 1999, www.agi-usa.org). A significant number of Christians have decided to adopt the world's position on sexual freedom instead of obeying God's standards of moral purity. That their search for intimacy results in loneliness, rejection, and heartbreak is no surprise.

This book is about relationships between men and women who have decided to take their friendships a step further and explore the possibilities of becoming serious dating partners. Relationships can be understood and their progression controlled so that heartaches can be avoided and lasting unions developed.

Care enough about your relationship to learn how it can be better.

1

Once Upon a Time

"When I first met Justin, it was just like a fairy tale," Ashley confided. "Love at first sight. Bliss. Everything . . . except the 'happily ever after' part. I'm not exactly sure what went wrong, but a few weeks later the magic was gone and we broke up."

"I wonder why relationships are so complicated," Robert complained. "I keep hearing that relationships take work. I guess I thought they just happened. Guy and girl meet, they fall in love, and get married. I never thought I'd have to *do* so much to build a lasting relationship."

"I know what you mean!" Amy shared. "*Working* at a relationship seems so unromantic! But in the last year, I've had three relationships that just fell apart. What does it take to make it work?"

A lot of single adults can identify with Ashley, Robert, and Amy, because relationships today are complicated and fragile. The pain of broken relationships is one most people have experienced at least once in their lives.

WHY ARE RELATIONSHIPS FRAGILE?

A loving, committed relationship between a guy and a girl can be the strongest unit of society, able to survive any problems, external or internal. Why, then, are many guy-girl relationships so fragile that they disintegrate in the face of seemingly minor challenges? Perhaps we do not take time to understand the dynamics of relationships or to develop appropriate relational skills.

Many people grow up believing that somewhere out there is one person *without* whom life will be forever incomplete and *with* whom life automatically will become blissfully perfect. The only perceived problem is finding and recognizing that *one-and-only*.

The myth is kept alive by thousands of romantic novels published and eagerly read each year, hundreds of sentimental movies with passionate scenes and tender music, and the promise of romantic fulfillment seen in almost every TV commercial. Magazines that line our newsstands hold up the ideal "playmate" companion or caring lover. We are surrounded by images of what true love looks like—how could such a popular idea be false?

Because it is!

There are not only no lifetime guarantees handed out at the altar but also a whole gamut of interpersonal emotions often interpreted as true love. Infatuation, sexual attraction, and romantic attachment make people feel so good, so fast that the experience is often labeled "true love" and expected to last forever. Yet true love is so much more than good feelings. It is the choice to invest in the life of someone, not only when it feels good but also when it doesn't.

Therefore, we see that romance is not the same as having an ongoing relationship. Relationships take time and work to develop and maintain; romance is a positive feeling toward another person. Romance without a relationship is a brief encounter at best. Still, people tend to seek romance, somehow believing that a lasting relationship will be part of the package. So in today's disposable society, couples hastily begin dating and easily go their separate ways at the first signs of conflict or disillusionment, as people search for the magic of instant love.

There are several reasons why people pursue the dream rather than take time to build lasting relationships:

A CASUAL SOCIETY

Society used to have very strict rules for male-female interactions. Time alone together was limited, dates carefully supervised. Because courting was only allowed after a man had asked permission to pay serious attention to a woman, the decision to begin "seeing" someone was not made impulsively. A broken engagement was not only a great tragedy but also grounds for a breach-of-promise lawsuit! People were expected to keep their commitments.

Today's casual lifestyle has given people almost total freedom to couple and uncouple at will. Doing what feels good will never build lasting relationships, because when conflicts arise between people what often feels good is walking out!

CHANGED SEXUAL MORES

Society in general no longer accepts biblical principles of sexual morality. Sex is considered a normal part of a dating relationship, and couples very often live together before or instead of marrying. Trends show people are meeting and becoming attracted to one another and sexually active without making a genuine commitment to a permanent relationship.

Because many Christians have fallen in with the current practices of sexual freedom, people choosing not to be involved sexually outside of marriage may find their dating options severely limited.

POOR RELATIONAL SKILLS

Because some people rely on the myth that the "perfect" guy or girl will guarantee a perfect marriage, they have not taken time to learn how to build a lasting relationship. To build a solid union means understanding how relationships develop, making a commitment to the relationship, and being willing to grow and develop as a partner in that relationship. Developing these skills takes lots of energy and practice, but the results are more than worth the effort.

REINFORCEMENT OF THE MYTH

Sometimes the love-at-first-sight fairy tale *seems* to come true. Inevitably, at least once in a lifetime, people fall in love and it is magical. It is everything the myth said it would be, and more! The world is a beautiful place, and all the love songs and romantic movies seem new and specifically just for "us."

Life becomes more exciting when we are in love. We glow. Being with our beloved is so wonderful that being apart is agony. The romantic high permeates our whole life, making the future seem brighter than ever before imagined! And we reason, since romance has turned out to be everything we hoped it would be, then it follows that the rest of the dream will also come true: This feeling will last forever!

Consequently, when reality hits us and we realize that he or she is less than "perfect," we become disillusioned about romance and blame ourselves or our partners for ruining the dream.

Unfortunately, the partner is often abandoned along with the myth, and the potential for a genuine relationship is not developed. But it need not be this way. *The key to building a strong and permanent relationship is understanding and controlling the progression of its development.*

BUT CAN RELATIONSHIPS REALLY BE UNDERSTOOD?

A relationship is an intimate connection between two people—the more intimate the interaction, the more significant the relationship. An acquaintance becomes a close friend as we increase the level of social intimacy and trust, and confide in that person. Among our many friends of the opposite sex, the one who becomes a serious dating partner is the one with whom we develop a greater level of emotional and /or physical intimacy.

INSTANT INTIMACY

We must be careful, however, of seeking "instant intimacy" and mistakenly assuming that such intimacy constitutes a lasting relationship. When two people begin to move toward one another in a relationship, they experience good feelings. In fact, the level of excitement rises in direct proportion to the speed with which they become intimately involved.

Karen shares, "The first night Jason and I went out for coffee, we sat and talked for hours. I felt like I'd known him forever! I told him things I'd never shared with anyone else, and he understood just how I felt. We saw each other every day after that first night. A week later he asked me to marry him, and I accepted. He was the most exciting guy I'd ever met! So sensitive. So understanding."

Jason remembers that initial excitement also. "I thought Karen was the most beautiful girl I'd ever seen. And she was so smart. That first night I kept wanting to reach out and touch her. She was so sweet. So sexy. I had to see her every day. When I discovered that she loved me, I knew she was the girl for me. We just had to spend the rest of our lives together!"

Karen had been out with other guys, and Jason had dated other girls; but because they rushed into an intimate relationship, they mistook excitement and romance for true love. Married just a month after they met, Karen and Jason soon discovered that the initial excitement cannot continue forever unless a solid friendship is the basis for the relationship. Four months later, disappointed and disillusioned, Karen and Jason separated and filed for divorce.

Karen and Jason are not unique, unfortunately. Many people seem to bounce from one relationship to another within short periods of time, never stopping long enough to develop strong, lasting relationships. Instead, once the thrill of one relationship begins to wear thin, a new romance is sought and the old one is discarded.

On the other hand, sometimes the movement from one involvement to another is to avoid commitment rather than to search for the excitement of a new interaction. Some may use this technique as a form of control, which prevents their getting too emotionally involved in relationships. Even if such a person were to marry, emotional commitment to the marriage would be lacking.

DEVELOPING INTIMACY

An interpersonal relationship progresses through various levels of intimacy. To illustrate our concepts about relationships, we will be using a model called "The Talley-Graph Interpersonal Relationship Development Model." The complete model is given in Chapter 10, but we will examine it one section at a time. Figure 1-1 shows the level of commitment and typical progression of a relationship from a guy's viewpoint.

At the friendship stage couples become familiar with each other on social, recreational, spiritual, intellectual, and communicative levels. A deep, enduring affection, built on similarities and mutual respect, develops. Friendships are more intellectual and less emotional than romantic love, and have no sexual connotations. Therefore, the standard for appropriate behavior in a friendship with a person of the opposite sex is doing only that which one would be comfortable doing with a friend of the same sex.

As a couple begins to date, and they want to experience increased closeness, their relationship progresses beyond the friendship stage to include emotional and physical intimacy. Physical intimacies such as holding hands and kissing are usually the first signs that a friendship has become a dating relationship. Soon one will see the couple hanging on to or touching each other, almost as a sign of physical possessiveness. By the time couples are inseparable, they often begin to exhibit emotional possessiveness and intimacy, as they long for, cry over, become defensive of, and totally committed to one another.

The next step, sexual intimacy, according to God's plan for us, should not occur until after the couple is married.

One of the complicating factors in the development of a relationship is that, regardless of age, guys and girls have a tendency to approach intimacy differently. For guys, physical intimacy often precedes emotional involvement; however, girls usually relate emotionally before they are physically close to a dating partner (see Figure 1-2). Obviously, if couples do not understand that these progressions are probably different for the guy and the girl, conflicts will arise.

If a girl believes that physical contact follows emotional intimacy, then she may assume her boyfriend to be as emotionally committed to the relationship as she is when he wants to spend time touching, holding, and kissing her. Because sexual intimacy is the next step in her progression, she may start expecting a marriage proposal once he initiates physical intimacy. Perfectly logical to her—possibly terrifying to him!

The relationship may end at this point. The guy, completely surprised by the depth of his partner's emotional attachment to him (just because he started kissing her and cuddling up on dates), may withdraw, explaining that he isn't ready for a serious relationship. Girls seem to have a nerve that connects their lips to their heart. When you kiss their lips, they have an emotional response. Guys, on the other hand, may not experience an emotional response to what they may consider casual kissing. The girl, upon discovering that her partner doesn't "love her as much as she loves him," may feel so rejected that she pulls back from all physical contact. From *his* perspective,

FIGURE 1-1

Level of Commitment and Progression of a Relationship

COMMITMENT MEN	PROGRESSION OF RELATIONSHIP	
SEXUAL	(MARRIAGE)	ADDICTED TO
		REGULAR
		PASSION
		PETTING
EMOTIONAL	DATING RELATIONSHIP	COMMITTED TO
		DEFENSIVE OF
		CRY OVER
		LONG FOR
PHYSICAL		ATTACHED TO
		CARESSING
		KISSING
		TOUCHING
SOCIAL	FRIENDSHIP	INTIMATE
		CLOSE
		CASUAL
		ACQUAINTANCE

FIGURE 1-2

Comparison of the Level of Commitment and the Progression Tendencies

COMMITMENT MEN	PROGRESSION OF RELATIONSHIP		COMMITMENT WOMEN	PROGRESSION OF RELATIONSHIP	
SEXUAL	(MARRIAGE)	ADDICTED TO	SEXUAL	(MARRIAGE)	ADDICTED TO
		REGULAR			REGULAR
		PASSION			PASSION
		PETTING			PETTING
EMOTIONAL	DATING RELATIONSHIP	COMMITTED TO	PHYSICAL	DATING RELATIONSHIP	ATTACHED TO
		DEFENSIVE OF			CARESSING
		CRY OVER			KISSING
		LONG FOR			TOUCHING
PHYSICAL		ATTACHED TO	EMOTIONAL		COMMITTED TO
		CARESSING			DEFENSIVE OF
		KISSING			CRY OVER
		TOUCHING			LONG FOR
SOCIAL	FRIENDSHIP	INTIMATE	SOCIAL	FRIENDSHIP	INTIMATE
		CLOSE			CLOSE
		CASUAL			CASUAL
		ACQUAINTANCE			ACQUAINTANCE

that means the relationship has reverted to mere friendship and he is free to develop a dating relationship with another person (see Figure 1-3).

Another result of having different progressions for men and women is that each responds differently to terminating a dating relationship. Obviously, the most significant pain comes from losing a relationship that has reached emotional intimacy, because more of oneself has been invested in the relationship. Girls, then, because they tend to become emotionally committed as the first step after friendship, may be hurt more deeply when a relationship breaks off. Guys, on the other hand, because they may not become emotionally involved until sometime after initiating physical intimacy, may be able to walk away more easily from a dating relationship in the early stages.

However, instead of breaking up because of a misunderstanding of how relationships develop, both partners may become emotionally attached much too quickly. The guy may initiate physical intimacy, and the woman may respond by making a hasty emotional commitment and expressing her love through physical contact. Soon, because the physical closeness is excitingly satisfying, the guy may make a marriage commitment with little or no emotional commitment on his part. The couple then decides to marry without having developed a deep emotional commitment.

True intimacy takes time to develop as trust must be built into each facet of a relationship by a series of shared experiences. These experiences test the assumptions made about each other. Neither a single moment of emotional "oneness" nor a sense of instant connection can substitute for complete emotional intimacy based on trust.

FIGURE 1-3

Comparison of Responses to Breakup of a Relationship from Men and Women If Different Progressions Are Followed

COMMITMENT MEN	PROGRESSION OF RELATIONSHIP	
SEXUAL	(MARRIAGE)	ADDICTED TO
		REGULAR
		PASSION
		PETTING
EMOTIONAL	DATING RELATIONSHIP	COMMITTED TO
		DEFENSIVE OF
		CRY OVER
		LONG FOR
PHYSICAL		ATTACHED TO
		CARESSING
		KISSING
		TOUCHING
SOCIAL	FRIENDSHIP	INTIMATE
		CLOSE
		CASUAL
		ACQUAINTANCE

COMMITMENT WOMEN	PROGRESSION OF RELATIONSHIP	
SEXUAL	(MARRIAGE)	ADDICTED TO
		REGULAR
		PASSION
		PETTING
PHYSICAL	DATING RELATIONSHIP	ATTACHED TO
		CARESSING
		KISSING
		TOUCHING
EMOTIONAL		COMMITTED TO
		DEFENSIVE OF
		CRY OVER
		LONG FOR
SOCIAL	FRIENDSHIP	INTIMATE
		CLOSE
		CASUAL
		ACQUAINTANCE

In this example, the relationship had progressed to the physical level where the couple had almost constant physical contact. For the guy, the return to the level of friendship was less of a change than for the girl, who had already made an emotional commitment to the relationship.

Recognizing and accepting the fact that physical and emotional intimacies tend to have different priorities for the guy and girl is the first step in resolving the problems those differences may cause. The second step is to exercise mutual patience. The girl must restrain her own emotions until her partner is ready to become emotionally committed to the relationship. A guy must refrain from physical intimacy until the girl's need for emotional involvement with and from him can be met. Neither partner should force the other partner: Decisions of commitment are personal and can only be made when the time and progression are comfortable.

ROMANCE VS. LOVE

Romance is fun! It is exciting! It is temporary! It has been described as

- eromania, a state of temporary madness
- a romanticized ego trip, unrecognized by either party
- a source of a new and wonderful self-image
- an instantaneous, but temporary, relief for loneliness
- a mutually shared dreamy vision of oneself and one's partner
- inflamed by external obstacles or controls
- a feeling to be enjoyed

On the other hand, true love is that bond which forms when the partners learn to give to each other, to put the other's best interests before their own, and to honestly accept each other as they are. According to 1 Corinthians 13, true love is

- essential to life itself
- patient
- constructive
- not possessive
- not anxious to impress
- not conceited or self-centered
- well mannered, behaving appropriately
- unselfish
- not easily upset
- not vengeful
- not happy over evil
- joyful in truth
- able to endure
- trusting
- forever!

What a standard! True love cannot suddenly appear. Instead, it must be carefully developed between two people committed to one another and to putting God first in their lives.

Don't mistake romance for love when developing a significant relationship with that guy or girl in your life. Take time to check out your expectations and assumptions about him or her as your relationship progresses toward possible total intimacy. Build a strong union at each stage of the relationship.

2

TIME: FRIEND OR FOE?

Answering the phone late one night, I (Jim) heard a slightly hysterical voice on the other end.

"What am I going to do?" Hayley, one of the girls in the college Bible study I taught, cried. "I don't know how it happened, but this guy I'm dating is really pressuring me to go to bed with him, and I just met him four days ago!"

Telling her to back up and start from the beginning, I asked if they had spent a lot of time together.

"Not really," she replied, then changed her answer as she told the story. It seems a new guy had come to work in the office where she had a job for the summer. Hayley had been assigned to train him in company policy and procedures, which meant they worked very closely all day (nine hours), getting acquainted in the process. They got along so well, they went out that first night (six hours). The next day after work (nine hours), he had come home with Hayley for dinner and an evening together (seven hours). During the third day at work (nine hours) and on their evening date (six hours), they continued to have a lot of fun together. After work (nine hours) on the fourth day, they didn't go out, but he began to exert heavy pressure for her to agree to have sex with him.

"You didn't go out, so did you talk on the phone?" I asked.

There was a slight pause. "Yeah. Three hours," Hayley admitted sheepishly. "I guess we're logging too many hours together, too soon, huh?"

Yes, Hayley. Almost sixty hours in four days is too close, too soon.

AN INTERPERSONAL RELATIONSHIP DEVELOPMENT MODEL

The progress of a relationship corresponds to the number of hours a couple spends alone together. For the purposes of visualization, imagine the development of the relationship over a period of several months (see Figure 2-1). Then consider how the hours spent alone together accumulate over those months (see Figure 2-2).

The Talley-Graph Model uses an arbitrary but, we believe, reasonable figure of three hundred hours alone together to show how a relationship develops from acquaintance to a sexually active involvement. As you look over the graph in Figure 2-3, you will notice that the curve of the relationship is controlled by the hours spent alone together.

People can be friends for years and accumulate time alone together without having a serious dating relationship. Accumulated time alone together becomes significant as a controlling factor when suddenly the couple discovers that they are more than friends.

FIGURE 2-1

Time Required to Develop a Relationship

COMMITMENT MEN	PROGRESSION OF RELATIONSHIP		MONTHS FIRST	SECOND	THIRD	FOURTH	FIFTH	SIXTH	SEVENTH
SEXUAL	(MARRIAGE)	ADDICTED TO							
		REGULAR							
		PASSION							
		PETTING							
EMOTIONAL	DATING RELATIONSHIP	COMMITTED TO							
		DEFENSIVE OF							
		CRY OVER							
		LONG FOR							
PHYSICAL		ATTACHED TO							
		CARESSING							
		KISSING							
		TOUCHING							
SOCIAL	FRIENDSHIP	INTIMATE							
		CLOSE							
		CASUAL							
		ACQUAINTANCE							

FIGURE 2-2

Accumulation of Time Alone Together Over a Period of Months

COMMITMENT MEN	PROGRESSION OF RELATIONSHIP		MONTHS FIRST	SECOND	THIRD	FOURTH	FIFTH	SIXTH	SEVENTH
SEXUAL	(MARRIAGE)	ADDICTED TO							
		REGULAR							
		PASSION							
		PETTING							
EMOTIONAL	DATING RELATIONSHIP	COMMITTED TO							
		DEFENSIVE OF							
		CRY OVER							
		LONG FOR							
PHYSICAL		ATTACHED TO							
		CARESSING							
		KISSING							
		TOUCHING							
SOCIAL	FRIENDSHIP	INTIMATE							
		CLOSE							
		CASUAL							
		ACQUAINTANCE							
			HOURS PER MONTH NUMBERS IN ( ) = ACCUMULATED TIME TOGETHER						
		IDEAL	12 (12)	18 (30)	25 (55)	35 (90)	50 (140)	70 (210)	90 (300)

FIGURE 2-3

The Talley-Graph Interpersonal Relationship Development Model

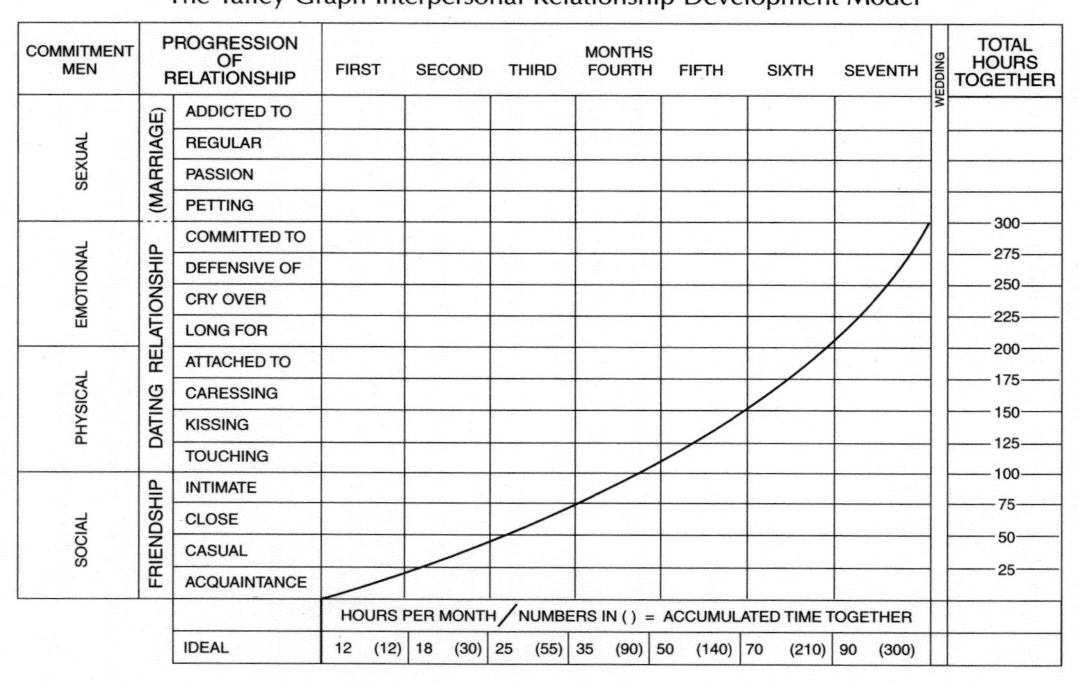

The actual number of hours two people can spend alone together before becoming sexually involved will, of course, vary from couple to couple, depending on the individuals involved. People who have been sexually active before may be in trouble long before they spend three hundred hours alone together. People whose schedules or geographic locations prevent their spending time together often find the three-hundred-hour mark to be insignificant because those hours were spread out over a period of several years. However, for the purposes of this model, the three-hundred-hour figure is used as the point at which a couple is likely to become sexually involved.

Also, the chart shows the "ideal" wedding date to be no earlier than the seventh month of a relationship, which means that the time alone together has been spaced out over several months. Seven months is just an average length of time couples spend dating seriously before marriage. A couple needs to share many experiences and see each other in a variety of settings and situations to really get to know one another. There must be time for romantic excitement to evaporate in the face of reality and for the strength of an emotional commitment to be given the test of time before a couple marries. Although the seventh month is by no means the "definitive month," marrying in less than six months after starting to date seriously is taking a risk that could very well end in a divorce.

CAN RELATIONSHIPS BE CONTROLLED?

Relationships are controllable and the controlling factor is ATAT: Accumulated Time Alone Together. Unless a relationship is controlled by the couple, it is likely to progress too quickly. Romance is addicting, and being together is so exciting that a couple will naturally want to spend more and more time alone together. Soon, no activity is satisfying without sharing it with the beloved, which further increases the couple's time together. Finally, they are inseparable. But by this time, just *being together* is not as exciting as it used to be, and physical intimacy is explored to recapture that initial thrill. Unless a couple sets limits for their relationship, they may discover they have drifted into sexual involvement without ever making a serious commitment to the relationship.

There are three variables to consider in order to keep a relationship under control so that the level of intimacy is developed in the proper order and sexual involvement is postponed until after the wedding: (1) attitude, (2) activities—what is done when the couple gets together, and (3) ATAT: accumulated time alone together.

ATTITUDE

Having an intimate relationship with the opposite sex is one of the most fulfilling experiences in life. However, our desires for such a relationship can sometimes become distorted so that our search for intimacy is a frantic, desperate cry for validation. "If no one loves me," we sometimes reason erroneously, "then I am unlovable." This attitude can lead to the belief that any relationship—good, bad, or indifferent—is better than no relationship at all, which is a very dangerous belief.

People using relationships with members of the opposite sex as sole sources of self-esteem tend to stay in relationships that are not healthy, even to the point of getting married, to avoid being alone.

Instead, as Christians, we need to approach serious dating relationships with the goal of developing in marriage the kind of intimacy Christ spoke of when He stated that a husband and wife become one flesh. This desire to build the best possible relationship leads a couple to work at fully exploring the various levels of intimacy in an appropriate sequence. It also results in a commitment to maintain biblical standards of behavior.

The appropriate attitude is one of obedience to God's laws and of respect for the spiritual development of the other, rather than a selfish desire to get as much as possible from the relationship. Choosing to keep a dating relationship under control will prevent a couple from getting carried away by passion to premature sexual intimacy. An obedient attitude allows a Christian couple to recognize and stop problem behaviors before the relationship is damaged. Partners choose to exercise the mutual patience required to allow the guy and the girl to become ready for physical and emotional intimacy. Natural sexual desires are acknowledged and accepted but not fulfilled during the dating relationship.

"Anna and I are both levelheaded, mature people. As long as we both love each other and want to have sex, why not? We're not hurting anyone!" Daniel says, echoing the attitude of thousands of dating couples.

But you would be hurting someone: God and yourselves. As Christians, we have certain responsibilities to meet. We are accountable for our actions and choices, to God, to ourselves, to our dating partners, and even to others.

TO GOD. Purity is a principle repeatedly emphasized in Scripture. In 1 Thessalonians 4:3–8 Paul says:

> It is God's will that you should be sanctified; that you should avoid sexual immorality; that each of you should learn to control his own body in a way that is holy and honorable, not in passionate lust like the heathen, who do not know God; and that in this matter no one should wrong his brother or take advantage of him. The Lord will punish men for all such sins, as we have already told you and warned you. For God did not call us to be impure, but to live a holy life. Therefore, he who rejects this instruction does not reject man but God, who gives you his Holy Spirit. (NIV; see also Matt. 5:27–28; 1 Cor. 6:9–20; Eph. 5:3–12; 2 Peter 2:9–16)

God says that sexual immorality is sin. Therefore, choosing to disobey God's rules on sexual purity disrupts a person's relationship with God and stunts spiritual growth.

Virginity is not renewable; celibacy is. Even if you have lost your virginity, at least regain your celibacy and determine to live a godly and moral life.

TO SELF. Authors Norman Wright and Marvin Inmon in the *Guidebook to Dating, Waiting, and Choosing a Mate* (Harvest House, 1978) give five advantages to not being sexually active before marriage.

1. There will be no guilt over having disobeyed God's laws.

2. There will be no fears of conceiving a child and having to decide what to do next: marry or have the child out of wedlock.

3. There will not be any comparing of one's spouse's sexual performance with that of past lovers.

4. The self-control learned by waiting for marriage will be transferable to any periods of absence from one's spouse.

5. The sexual satisfaction shared with only each other brings excitement to the marriage.

Another important reason to abstain is that physical intimacy within a relationship requires a significant investment of self. Expressing all of one's passion for and love of one's partner by the fantastic act of making love creates a special togetherness apart from the rest of the world. That special oneness we feel when holding and touching each other is a precious part of an intimate relationship. And with sexual intimacy comes complete vulnerability. Every relationship that we allow to go into premature sexual involvement takes a piece of our soul and distorts more of our character.

Because a person may have several serious dating relationships before marriage, including sexual intimacy as part of dating would mean sharing one's innermost self with several people. The special sharing that is part of an exclusive sexual relationship is lost. Many couples who divorce after many years of marriage will confirm that their problems started with premarital sex and grew into irreconcilable differences. Sports figures and rock stars who claim thousands of sexual encounters before and even during their marital relationships are examples of how unfulfilling these choices can be.

TO ONE'S PARTNER. Although ultimately we do not determine the actions of others, we are not acting in a caring and responsible way when we tempt or encourage another person to sin. Even if we were to decide to disobey God's laws, we do not have the right to encourage or pressure another person to make that choice. Also, since it takes two people to have sexual intercourse, our own obedience can keep our partner from sinning, even when they are not strong enough to resist temptation on their own.

Therefore, it is our responsibility to our dating partner to abstain from making love before marriage. If we make that commitment, then we must also refrain from doing those things that sexually arouse both ourselves and our partners to the point of giving in to temptation.

TO OTHERS. "I don't mean to pry into your business, Ken," Dennis commented one day at work, "but how do you and your girlfriend handle the fact that you live together? I mean, I thought you were really religious and all that!"

No matter what standards the world sets for itself, Christians are still expected to have high moral standards. When Christians break God's laws, their witness is damaged and dismissed as meaningless. The first step in controlling a relationship is to choose to have a positive and obedient attitude.

ACTIVITIES

The second way to control a relationship is to choose carefully how time together will be spent. Some activities help build relationships; other choices may be unwise. A whole Saturday spent at your sister's softball tournament is much less dangerous than several hours spent cuddling and kissing passionately in a darkened room while listening to romantic music. Some activities or locations that are acceptable at the beginning of the relationship may soon become unacceptable as the relationship continues. Going over to her place alone may be okay in the early stages, but if the physical relationship gets out of control you may need to decide that certain places are off-limits later in the relationship.

Although physical contact is a perfectly natural part of a serious dating relationship, most of the time alone together should be spent *doing* something, such as sharing ideas, working on projects, participating in sports, or sharing spiritually.

ATAT: ACCUMULATED TIME ALONE TOGETHER

The third factor in controlling relationships is limiting the time spent alone together. This, of course, feels completely opposite of the natural desire to spend every available moment with each other. Unless a couple limits the number of hours spent together, they can quickly move from a once-a-week date to an every evening and all weekend relationship. Under those conditions, the hours add up rapidly. For example:

A. THE ONCE-A-WEEK DATE

7:00 P.M. to 11:00 P.M. = 4 hours per date = a year and half to reach 300 hours alone together (see Figure 2-1)

B. THE EVERY-NIGHT DATE

7:00 P.M. to 11:00 P.M. = 4 hours per date x 7 nights = 28 hours per week = 2 ½ months to reach 300 hours alone together

C. THE ALL-WEEKEND DATE

8:00 A.M. to 11:00 P.M. = 15 hours per day x 2 days = 30 hours per week = 2 ½ months to reach 300 hours together

A combination of any of the above can quickly reduce the number of weeks it takes to accumulate three hundred hours alone together.

Please note that not only must the total number of hours spent alone together be controlled but also how those hours are grouped. Too many consecutive hours spent alone together can weaken resistance to sexual temptation. Several shorter dates are safer than one *very long* date. Long time periods alone together run down your moral batteries, and you'll need time apart to recharge your resistance to immorality. Too much time together is like leaving the car lights on—when the time comes for you to leave, you can't start the car.

Another reason for limiting the time spent together is that in spite of the fact that a love relationship seems to be the most important thing in our lives at the time, other things do require attention. We still need time alone, time with our friends and families, time with God, and time to keep up with the duties of daily living. Neglecting any of these other tasks and interactions can cause us a lot of pain later on.

BEING ACCOUNTABLE FOR THE RELATIONSHIP

The first step in taking responsibility for the relationship is to sit down, discuss, and agree on the limits for the relationship. Next, review the agreement with a pastor or a spiritual leader in the church and make a commitment to live within the agreement.

One way to formalize the commitment is to put it in writing and have all three parties sign the agreement. A sample agreement is given at the end of this chapter.

If, after signing such a commitment, both of you pray together with your spiritual leader and confirm your decision before God, you will be less likely to change your minds impulsively because of aroused passions later on. Agreeing to be accountable to a spiritual leader is a strong deterrent for exceeding limits set for the relationship.

No plan is of value without follow-up and evaluations to verify that the plan is working. So, after you have set limits for the relationship you will want to develop a way of checking on yourselves. You might want to record the time you spend together. As a rule of thumb, time spent talking on the phone is logged after the first half hour. Time together with others (group time) is logged after dividing by 4. Figure 2-4 is an example of a monthly time chart.

ALREADY INVOLVED

A significant number of couples—even Christians—are sexually involved before marriage. One reason for this high level of sexual activity is that many couples invest a significant number of hours alone together without considering the consequences of such actions. A second reason is the failure of Christian couples to make an absolute commitment to the Lord to say *no* to the temptation to sin sexually. So, they depend on the feelings of the moment and run into trouble.

A couple who is already sexually involved, or who become so aroused they ignore their commitment and go to bed together,

FIGURE 2-4
Monthly Time Chart

HIS NAME ____________ MONTH ____________ GOAL ____________ HER NAME ____________

CALENDAR DATE DAY OF WEEK	1	2	3	4	5	6	7	8	9	10	11	12	13	14	15	16	17	18	19	20	21	22	23	24	25	26	27	28	29	30	31
6																															
7																															
AM 8																															
9																															
10																															
11																															
NOON 12																															
1																															
2																															
3																															
4																															
5																															
PM 6																															
7																															
8																															
9																															
10																															
11																															
MIDNIGHT 12																															
1																															
2																															
AM 3																															
4																															
5																															
SUB-TOTALS																															
ONE-ON-ONE																															
GROUP																															
INTERNET/PHONE																															

x ONE-ON-ONE
o GROUP
· PHONE/INTERNET (OVER 1/2 HOUR)

EXAMPLE

DATE	1	2	3	4	5
DAY	M	T	W	T	F
6	x		·	o	·
7	x		·	o	·
8	o	x	x	o	·
AM 9	o	x	x	o	x
10	·	x	x	·	o
ONE-ON-ONE	2	2	3	0	1
GROUP	2	0	0	4	1
INTERNET/PHONE	1	1	2	1	3

TOTAL HOURS

ONE-ON-ONE ____________
GROUP ÷ 4 = ____________
PHONE/INTERNET ____________
____

MONTHLY TOTAL ____________
PREVIOUS TOTAL ____________
NEW TOTAL ____________

MONTHLY
____
____
____

will want to get the relationship back under control. Although they could move their wedding date up and get married, or go to the other extreme and quit seeing each other, a better alternative is to reflect on the situation and plan how to prevent another occurrence. They may want to consider

- reading and paraphrasing 1 Corinthians 10:13.

- listing ways of escape God provided that were ignored. Couples are often surprised when they think back to the situation and realize just how many interruptions or escapes were provided (the phone ringing, a friend dropping by, or even difficulties finding opportunities to be alone). Acknowledging to God (and to our partner) that we did ignore these escapes allows us to be forgiven and set free to choose to be more responsible the next time.

- identifying steps that could be taken to help prevent a recurrence. Time spent alone together may need to be reduced for a while. However, because the goal is to regain control of the progression of the relationship and not to terminate it, communication should not stop. Time spent together with others or talking on the phone can increase, or the couple may want to e-mail one another expressing, their thoughts and feelings.

Once the relationship is under control again, the couple may choose to return to spending time alone together. However, they will want to plan safe activities that will minimize the risk of becoming sexually involved again.

RELATIONSHIP COUNSELING

"I've never heard of trying counseling to improve or save a relationship," Todd said. "To save a marriage, yes. Or even the usual premarital counseling that pastors often require. But relationship counseling?"

Yes! Your pastor, a spiritual elder, or a professional counselor can provide a valuable third person's view of what is going on in a relationship. Problem solving can become more objective and logical, which helps the couple develop a mature style of conflict resolution. But perhaps the counselor's most important function is assisting the couple to develop accountability. Relationship instruction is just pre-premarital. It is to help the relationship stay on a moral course until the couple can decide if they want to consider marriage; after the proposal they can shift to the regular premarital counseling. (I [Jim] offer a resource titled *Relationship Instruction*, which is a separate workbook partially outlined in the back of this book. The complete workbook can be ordered from *www.drtalley.com*)

ANY TIME IS THE RIGHT TIME!

Counseling is appropriate at any point in a relationship but especially when the couple is ready to become physically (not sexually) and emotionally intimate.

People may go for counseling or take a class on relationships before they enter into a friendship. Principles, concepts, expectations, and potential dangers are all easier to learn and accept *before* we become emotionally involved with a specific dating partner. In fact, responses to advice or counseling become less positive in direct proportion to the level of involvement in the relationship (see Figure 2-5). During the early stages of a friendship, couples are usually open and responsive to advice on how best to keep the relationship under control and what to expect as a result of specific behaviors.

When a relationship gets into trouble, counseling can sometimes assist the couple in resolving their problems. If the trouble is sexual involvement, then reducing time alone together and improving other aspects of the relationship are usually the two most successful interventions.

Couples can often regain control of the relationship after a single "heavy petting" session. However, if there is no counseling, they often move into consistent sexual involvement. As indicated in Figure 2-5, there is a point of no return, after which a couple tends to be closed to counsel and are virtually committed to immorality unless the wedding is imminent.

Counseling can assist couples in affecting a reconciliation after a breakup if both parties are willing to commit to making the relationship work. And a counselor can help people in the aftermath of a broken relationship to understand what went wrong and to prepare to avoid similar problems in future relationships.

WHO DOES RELATIONSHIP COUNSELING?

Finding the right counselor may not be as easy as opening a phone book and ordering a pizza. Possible counselors include pastors, youth group leaders, college or single adult directors, psychologists, and family and marriage counselors. The financial costs of counseling will range from free to expensive, and each

FIGURE 2-5

Thought Response to Authority or Counsel at Different Levels of Intimacy

MEN		PROGRESSION OF RELATIONSHIP	KEY POINTS	TOTAL HOURS	THOUGHT RESPONSE TO AUTHORITY OR COUNSEL
SEXUAL	(MARRIAGE)	ADDICTED TO			
		REGULAR			
		PASSION			
		PETTING			
EMOTIONAL	DATING RELATIONSHIP	COMMITTED TO		300	REBEL
		DEFENSIVE OF		275	RUN AWAY
		CRY OVER	LINE OF NO RETURN	250	AVOID
		LONG FOR		225	DISOBEY
PHYSICAL		ATTACHED TO		200	ARGUE
		CARESSING		175	DISAGREE
		KISSING		150	QUESTION
		TOUCHING	START COUNSELING	125	WONDER
SOCIAL	FRIENDSHIP	INTIMATE		100	CONSIDER
		CLOSE		75	RESPOND
		CASUAL		50	LISTEN
		ACQUAINTANCE		25	

couple will have to decide just what price or priority they will assign to saving or improving their relationship. (One note: Do seek out a Christian who has a high view of Scripture and is using God's Word as the basis of his or her counseling. Many Christians have fallen into the trap of secular "me first" psychology.)

RELATIONSHIPS ARE PRECIOUS

A close relationship with a member of the opposite sex is a most precious treasure. People who go through life without developing such a relationship usually come to a point where they feel their entire lives have been worthless. We all need to love and be loved in return. God saw that need when He created Adam, and He knew that what Adam lacked was someone with whom to share. So God created Eve.

If relationships are that significant and necessary to us, then they are also valuable enough to be accountable for and to spend time, energy, and even money on. If we do not, we risk the failure and loss of our relationships.

Agreement to Build a Genuine Friendship

Friendship is the essential foundation for an enduring relationship. Therefore, we desire through our friendship to

- promote spiritual maturity through encouraging one another in worship and service to Jesus Christ.
- develop *agape* love.
- learn to control physical, emotional, and mental habits, thereby giving our friendship a healthy environment in which to grow.
- build trust, integrity, and openness.

This agreement will cover a period of _______months, from _______ to ________, during which time we will control the speed with which our relationship develops.

Our goals for the period of time covered by this agreement are:

1. ____
2. ____
3. ____
4. ____
5. ____
6. ____
7. ____
8. ____

In order to reach these goals, we agree to:

1. Limit our time alone together to ____ hours per month.

   (This means to average _____ hours per date and _____ dates per week.)

2. Spend our time together doing such things as

   ____

   ____

   ____

   ____

3. We agree to avoid activities or situations that might be detrimental to our relationship, such as

   ____

   ____

   ____

   ____

We commit ourselves under the authority of God to be accountable for the terms of this agreement to ______________________________, our spiritual leader and adviser.

Signed________________________________Date____________

Signed________________________________Date____________

Signed________________________________Date____________

3

TOGETHERNESS IS NOT ENOUGH!

Jake and Wendy spend a lot of time together. For the last few months they have settled into a comfortable routine. Three or four times a week Jake comes over to Wendy's apartment after work; they order in or prepare a simple dinner; and they spend the evening watching television together. Jake usually is intensely involved in the shows, and Wendy often flips through magazines or catches up on some work while listening to the programs. They seldom talk during the evening beyond casual questions about one another's day.

Most of their friends consider Jake and Wendy to be involved seriously, and in fact, they have been considering marriage. Yet Jake and Wendy really don't know each other!

Kate and Sam work out together several times a week, but talking at the gym is minimal.

Michael and Julie have three out of five of their classes together, but after class, their conversations center on their homework or studying for their next test.

None of these pairs are intimate friends in the true sense, because togetherness alone is not enough to move people from acquaintanceship to intimacy. Therefore, two people who meet and feel attracted to each other cannot assume that just following their natural desires to *be* together is sufficient to propel the friendship toward a genuinely intimate relationship.

In the early stages of a relationship, being together feels so good and is so satisfying that couples don't always feel a need to work at building a foundation for a lasting relationship. But if a relationship is based purely on feelings, just being together will soon lose its magic. Either an increase in physical intimacy will occur in an attempt to recapture the good feelings or the relationship will be broken off. The alternative is to develop a lasting relationship by getting to know and appreciate one another and by sharing each other's lives.

Be Open

One of the best aspects of having a new friend is rediscovering ourselves as we tell stories about our pasts, our accomplishments, our dreams, and our fiascos. But just sharing facts about ourselves is only one part of getting to know one another. More significant is the sharing of our feelings, our inner responses to what has happened, is happening, or might happen in our lives.

Often we find it easier to share positive emotions than negative ones (such as anger, hurt, frustration, fear, resentment), because we fear being rejected. And yet, because everyone experiences both negative and positive emotions, people recognize that those who do not admit to having negative responses are being less than honest.

A second problem with suppressing negative feelings is that suppression is only temporary. Eventually, when the pressure builds, an explosion is likely to occur. Sharing honestly and discussing negative feelings calmly never damage a relationship as much as an explosion of suppressed feelings. Keeping negative feelings pent-up inside is indicative of either a lack of trust of one's partner or a nonacceptance of self. Both trust and self-acceptance are essential to a solid friendship.

The process of giving and sharing feedback with a dating partner is one of the most critical aspects of developing a genuinely loving relationship. Through feedback we learn about ourselves, because feedback is basically information about how others feel about us, what they perceive in us, and how they respond to our behaviors.

LEARNING TO BE OPEN

In *Why Am I Afraid to Tell You Who I Am?* (Thomas More, 1995), John Powell names five levels of communication: cliché conversations, reporting facts about others, my ideas and judgments, my feelings, and complete emotional and personal communication. A couple who wants their relationship to last and to be special will want to use all levels of communication, particularly the last three. They will need to overcome many obstacles, such as not talking at all, not listening, not being honest, being defensive, not sharing feelings, arguing rather than sharing, avoiding confrontation, criticizing, interrupting, making assumptions, and ignoring problems instead of resolving issues as they arise.

Being open is a challenge, and sometimes a risk, but it is an absolute necessity for a relationship to work. If we had to overcome these obstacles to openness, in our own strength, we might fail. However, we have a God "who is able to do immeasurably more than all we ask or imagine, according to his power that is at work within us" (Eph. 3:20 NIV).

With the power of the Holy Spirit within us, we have the ability to change and grow!

BE ACTIVE

Just being together does not contribute to the emotional depth of a relationship. Depth comes from doing things together. As people participate together in sports, projects, or other activities, they learn a lot about each other's levels of frustration, enjoyment, learning ability, and energy patterns. They discover shared and individual interests while adding excitement to their own lives. Therefore, a dating couple may want to explore many different interests and activities.

Jack and Emily served as after-school tutors at their local literacy center. Helen and Caleb worked with Habitat for Humanity. Paul and Julie built some bookshelves for her apartment. Sandra and Ray joined a frisbee golf team. Jill and Ed assembled a collection of U2 memorabilia by scouring music stores and researching on-line.

As couples share together in activities and projects, they grow closer together and their relationship is deepened.

CONFRONT IN LOVE

"Carmen and I have been dating for six months, and we've never had a disagreement about anything. We're perfect for each other," Kyle declared happily.

That may be true, but it is more likely that Kyle and Carmen have not developed a problem-solving system that will carry them through the realities of a long-term, close relationship—because conflict is inevitable. People are individuals, not carbon copies of one another. As my friend Jim Weatherford says, "If two people agree on everything, one of them isn't necessary." Therefore, no matter how similar a couple's tastes, ideas, or opinions, there will eventually be areas of conflict. Learning to resolve conflicts without destroying the relationship is an important skill.

James Fairfield in *When You Don't Agree* (Herald Press, 2001) suggests five responses to conflict: withdraw, win, yield, compromise, and resolve.

WITHDRAW

Sally withdraws. At the first sign of conflict, she turns on the television, changes the subject, or goes for a drive. Even though withdrawing temporarily to sort out one's thoughts and feelings may be a valuable technique, continued use of withdrawal as a response to conflict is destructive to a relationship.

Withdrawal says, "Our relationship isn't worth or can't withstand a confrontation." Consistent withdrawal indicates a giving up on the relationship and predicts an eventual turning to other relationships for the affirming interaction we all need. The payoff of withdrawal may be the avoidance of confrontation, but the price is loss of the relationship.

WIN

Pete must always win! Whether playing a game, making a bet, or stating an argument, he must not lose! In the heat of the contest, Pete loses sight of people and relationships as his desire to win takes over. On those rare occasions when Pete does not win, he is a poor loser, often sulking or pouting.

Winners usually appear to be successful in life because they do achieve. But their relationships tend to be superficial or short-lived, because their victories are often at the expense of the ideas, opinions, values, feelings, and rights of others. The payoff is the feeling of victory; the price is lost relationships.

YIELD

Patty's style is to give in to Eric's ideas rather than to argue or discuss issues. Yielding stops the conflict, but it does not build mutual trust and respect if one partner does most of the yielding. The person who does the yielding does not feel valued by his or her partner, whose victories are always at the yielder's expense.

The payoff is peace in the relationship, but the price is one-sided interaction, in which one partner's self-esteem is diminished.

COMPROMISE

In a compromise, nobody wins or loses. Both make some concessions to the other's point of view or desires, because the relationship is considered more important than the confrontation.

The payoff is a working relationship and an acceptable solution, but the price is *always* settling for less than best.

RESOLVE

The resolve (or consensus) style of problem solving is the ideal but also the one that requires the most work to achieve. Partners acknowledge the conflict and work together to find a solution. As Christians, we have heavenly resources available to help us resolve our earthly conflicts. James told those who lack wisdom to ask God, who gives it generously (see James 1:5). Jesus said, "The Counselor, the Holy Spirit, whom the Father will send in my name, will teach you all things" (John 14:26 NIV; see also 1 Cor. 2:10–16).

As alternatives for resolving the conflict are brought to mind, they are explored and evaluated. Together, the best alternative is selected. The difference between *compromise* and *resolve* is that in a compromise both people have a proposed solution to a problem even before they discuss the problem. Starting from two different points of view, they negotiate a settlement, which is a combination of the two proposed solutions.

In the resolve style, both of you discuss needs, problems, and many possible solutions. Because neither starts with a specific alternative to argue for or sacrifice, there is no compromise. Finding the final solution is a joint effort. The resolve style acknowledges the value of both the relationship and the issue—and neither is sacrificed in the process.

This approach to problem solving requires a significant investment of time and emotional and mental energies, so it is not practical for solving every little conflict that arises. But it is the best method for the major issues.

The payoff is an improved relationship and a great solution; the price is the investment of time and self.

People will use each of these styles at different times in their lives with different people. But in a lasting relationship, the predominant style will be *resolve*. This style requires skills in listening, sharing, accepting, being flexible, and being creative—skills learned through frequent practice. The *resolve* style is not a natural style because all of us have an innate desire for power and winning. (Sometimes "winning" is giving in because that results in control.) However, only by using the *resolve* style can we be winners in the best sense of the word.

Identifying areas of conflict may be as simple as waiting for differences in opinions, values, or desires to arise. Or you may want to develop a list of topics to discuss over a period of time for the specific purpose of determining where your ideas and values differ.

The important thing is for problem resolution to occur in an attitude of love so that you grow closer through resolving a problem. Conflict can be divisive or beneficial, depending on how it is handled.

SHARE SPIRITUALLY

Sharing at all levels brings a couple closer together; however, sharing spiritually has the greatest impact on the quality and depth of a relationship. Suggestions for sharing on a spiritual level include

- sharing what God is teaching you
- discussing individual spiritual struggles and victories
- praying with and for one another
- studying the Word together
- attending Bible study and worship services together and discussing main points afterwards
- serving together by coteaching a Bible study, cosponsoring a youth group, cochairing a committee participating in community services at rest homes, jails, hospitals, or missions

Sharing in another's spiritual life helps us feel encouraged in our own growth. When you as dating partners share spiritually, you will find it easier to turn the relationship over to God and to let Him draw you together in His time. Sometimes when the relationship doesn't seem to be developing fast enough, people find it difficult to be patient. But as the saying goes, "The only thing worse than waiting is wishing you had!"

Deciding that any dating relationship will include sharing spiritually precludes dating non-Christians. Although a Christian since she was five years old, and in spite of being well-versed in Scripture, twenty-six-year-old Sandra had married a nonbeliever five years before. Although she and her husband were almost perfectly suited in every other aspect of their lives, Sandra expressed the agony of being unable to share the most precious part of her life with her mate—her personal relationship with the Lord. This awareness had only become acute in the last year when, after a near fatal swimming accident, Sandra had renewed her fellowship with the Lord.

"You've got to listen to me!" she told her younger sister one day. "Don't go out with guys who aren't Christians. I learned the hard way. I never planned to marry a non-Christian. I thought, *Show me a Christian I like and I'll date him!* But I didn't meet one, so I dated anyone I wanted to. Naturally, since I only dated non-Christians, I fell in love with and married one. And I can't tell you how it hurts to love my husband so much and to be spiritual opposites. You fall in love with and marry the kind of person you date. So don't take a chance! Wait for God to bring a Christian man into your life!"

In 2 Corinthians 6:14 we are told not to be unequally yoked with nonbelievers because there can be no genuine fellowship.

"Evangelistic dating" is not the way to win people to Christ, even though that sometimes might happen. More often, though, a believer's spiritual life weakens when dating non-Christians.

THE TOTAL RELATIONSHIP

Getting to know one another in a variety of settings, sharing intellectually, recreationally, and spiritually keeps a relationship balanced and vibrantly alive.

Just being together isn't enough! Relationships take a lot of hard work!

4

Absence Is Not for Pining

"Limiting my time alone with John doesn't do any good, because when we are apart I spend every single minute thinking about him!" Amanda confessed after a seminar on controlling relationships. "When we're not together I don't function well. I'm always waiting around for his calls or for him to come over. So we might as well be together! Besides, we're in love, and I wouldn't want it any other way!"

Sounds as if Amanda has an even bigger problem than controlling her relationship with John. This problem is called codependency, and it is very destructive to relationships. The longer she takes to realize that John cannot be her whole life, the more out of balance her life will become. *People are not ready to have a new relationship or to get married until they are content to be single*.

All too many guys and girls experience a great deal of anxiety about the possibility that they might remain single for the rest of their lives. This anxiety causes them to behave in ways that are frequently nonproductive. And yet, they could discover the secret inner peace found in Philippians 4:5–11.

Paul tells us to control our thought lives by focusing on the positives and following his example. He concludes verse 11 by saying, "I have learned to be content whatever the circumstances" (NIV).

PUTTING GOD FIRST

"I can really tell a difference on those days when I start the morning talking with God!" Kristi says.

Spending those few minutes each morning talking to God and listening to Him can give us a positive attitude all day, if we truly commit the day to Him and trust Him to work in our lives. Just as we need nutritious food each day to give us physical energy, we also need daily spiritual food to strengthen our inner persons. That spiritual input comes from reading and meditating on the Word, from talking with God in prayer, and from living obedient, service-oriented lives.

Spending time with other believers, attending Bible studies and worship services, and using your gifts and resources to help others are additional ways to develop your spiritual life. But since the relationship we have with God is personal and individual, much of our spiritual growth comes from spending time alone communing with Him.

Thus, another focus for time spent apart from a dating partner is your relationship with God. If we applied the Talley-Graph concept to our relationship with God, some of us might be surprised that we are only at an acquaintance level with Him because of the limited time we spend alone with Him.

MY ALL-IN-ALL

No one person can be another's "all-in-all." To expect one person to meet our every social and emotional need is not only unrealistic but also unfair. Instead, we need a well-developed social network that includes a variety of friends, each with his or her own unique personality.

Intimate friends share each other's innermost thoughts, fears, failures, and hopes. They relate at the deepest spiritual and emotional levels, supporting each other during times of crisis and pain. Their joy in each other's success is genuine. Everybody needs one or two intimate friends. However, because of the significant investment of ourselves that it takes to support a truly intimate friendship, we cannot have many friends on this level.

Close friends are somewhat less intimate, yet they may spend a lot of time doing things together. They know each other fairly well and play a significant social role for one another. Close friends, however, tend to have a more limited emotional involvement in each other's lives than intimate friends do, because they share more external activities than inner thoughts. So, as a result, we usually have more close friends than intimate ones.

Casual friends spend time together occasionally because of some shared interest or mutual friends. We need many casual friends in our lives.

A complete social network includes these three types of friends, of both sexes, all age ranges, and both married and single people represented at each level of friendship. Therefore, time apart from a dating partner can be spent developing or enjoying these other friendships.

FAMILY TIME

Often after leaving the family home and establishing your own lifestyle, you will develop a new appreciation for your family. Brothers and sisters, no longer just rival siblings, may become friends. You may learn to relate to your parents in a more positive and accepting way. And your parents also, relieved of feeling responsible for your actions, can begin to relate to you adult to adult.

So building or rebuilding relationships with your family is another way to invest the time spent apart from your dating partner.

ALONE, BUT NOT LONELY

"For the first time in my life I'm beginning to enjoy being alone once in a while!" Darin shared one night during a coffee and conversation time sponsored by his college group.

Several others nodded their heads in agreement. Time alone need not be a lonely experience! It is an important opportunity to engage in any number of restful self-indulgent and just-for-me activities.

Tanya sometimes spends a whole evening reading a novel, escaping to another time and place for a few hours. Sam watches his favorite sports—something his girlfriend doesn't enjoy. Glenda works on her hobby, fashion design. Earl listens to music. Dana makes sure she has at least forty minutes a day all to herself so she can physically and emotionally relax. Peter gets in extra sleep.

Time alone can become so important that once people get over their fears of being lonely, they often begin to set aside time for themselves deliberately. *In fact, those who cannot tolerate being alone at all need to take a look at why they don't enjoy their own company.*

REACHING GOALS

Another way to use time away from a dating partner is to get involved in goal-reaching activities. These might include evening classes toward a college degree, workshops of special interests, personal growth seminars, learning a new sport, or picking up an old hobby.

LIVING A BALANCED LIFE

Perhaps the key thought for this chapter is that people need to work toward achieving balance in their lives, not only in the area of relationships but also in all other aspects of life. We all know people whose lives are out of balance. For example: Rhonda thinks, talks about, and lives only for her career; Michael spends all of his free time playing virtual reality games; William is a partygoer, out every night with different friends.

When one aspect of our lives becomes overemphasized, the balance is disturbed and soon one's whole life becomes lopsided. Of course, there will often be times when one priority throws our entire lives out of balance for a short time until the desired objective has been achieved. Just before finals week most college students call a halt to any activities not directly related to a frantic review of the semester's notes and textbooks. But such extremes are time limited, and after a few days of rest and relaxation once exams are over, life returns to normal.

Often we can function for years, even with obvious imbalances in our lives. But the old saying "All work and no play makes Jack a dull boy" has a message for us. We need to accept the many facets of our personalities and give attention to developing well-rounded lifestyles.

Achieving balance does not require spending an exactly equal amount of time or energy developing each area of your life; rather each aspect is given reasonable attention. For example, one area to examine is how energy is expended. Different occupations involve specific types of energy. Logging, construction, ditch-digging, and coaching sports all require physical energy. Marriage counselors and pastors expend a great deal of emotional energy. Planning, managing, teaching, and bookkeeping involve primarily intellectual energy.

Yet people in each of these professions need balance, so different types of after-hours activities are sought. Laborers may seek intellectual stimulation and emotional involvement. An accountant may desire to be physically and emotionally active. People in the helping professions often want to do something involving physical or intellectual energy.

CHRIST SET AN EXAMPLE

In spite of the fact that He knew He was only going to have a little over three years to fulfill His earthly mission, Christ Himself set an example of living a balanced life. His time was divided among the multitudes, friends, disciples, His special intimates from among the disciples, Himself, and His Father. He sometimes feasted; other times He fasted. He served and allowed Himself to be served. He traveled, rested, taught, worked miracles, and held children. He shared and took time to listen. Sometimes He cried, and other times He rejoiced with His friends. He took time to appreciate the beauty of nature. He was physically, emotionally, and intellectually active, while at the same time being single-minded in His desire to do His Father's will.

BE HEALTHY

An important reason to seek balance is that our bodies do not respond well to excesses. Overeating causes obesity, which results in heart problems, impaired circulation, and any number of other physical malfunctions. Overworking can result in heart attacks and hypertension. Too many life changes in a short period of time set up a stress overload manifested in a variety of physical symptoms, such as insomnia, headaches, colds, flu, allergies, impotence, ulcers, colitis, asthma, dermatitis, hypertension, premature aging, bronchitis, emphysema, diabetes, heart disease, tuberculosis, and even cancer.

The body needs a balanced approach to life so that it can function on a fairly even keel and maintain its good health.

BE INTERESTING!

People whose lives are in balance are in a position to contribute more to a dating relationship than is someone whose life is "lopsided." Well-balanced people are interested in other people, new ideas, and various activities; therefore they are fascinating themselves! They rarely feel out of place in new situations, because they have learned how to relate to all types of people.

So in spite of the fact that people usually want to spend most of their time with their dating partners, time apart can be one of the best things you do for your relationship.

5

One of a Kind

As dating partners seek to develop a committed relationship, a positive self-image becomes increasingly important. People who secretly hate themselves cannot truly accept love when it is given. Neither can they believe that their love is of any lasting value to anyone. Therefore, building a positive self-image is essential to a successful, intimate relationship with a member of the opposite sex.

One of the reasons some people have difficulty developing a positive self-concept is that they have a misconception of just what self-esteem is all about.

It is not believing that you are perfect. *It is not* egotism. *It is not* complacent smugness. *It is not* being blind to your weaknesses.

A positive self-image involves

- honest self-appraisal, including consideration of the opinions of others

- an acceptance of yourself, as God created you
- recognition that, with God's help, you can change destructive behavior, sinful attitudes, and personality weaknesses
- choosing to make those changes, one at a time

YOU ARE UNIQUE

All too often people refuse to accept themselves because they don't want to be different from everyone else. People subscribe to popular beliefs, dress in the latest fashions, or follow silly fads in an effort to fit in with the crowd. They become imitations rather than individuals.

Yet their efforts are all in vain, for underneath the superficiality of outward conformity, no two people are truly alike. Each one of us is a unique creation, designed and made by God Himself. David says,

> For Thou didst form my inward parts;
> Thou didst weave me in my mother's womb.
> I will give thanks to Thee,
> for I am fearfully and wonderfully made;
> Wonderful are Thy works,
> And my soul knows it very well.
> My frame was not hidden from Thee,
> When I was made in secret,
> And skillfully wrought in the depths of the earth.
> Thine eyes have seen my unformed substance;
> And in Thy book they were all written,

The days that were ordained for me,
When as yet there was not one of them.
(Ps. 139:13–16 NASB; see also Job 10:8–10)

Denying our individuality is to some degree a rejection of God's design for our lives. How we develop that design has a lot to do with our response to the experiences of daily living, as described in the following poem:

THE SEA OF LIFE

The iridescent sand
Lies gleaming and white
Her complexion washed
By the cleansing tide,
Each wave with its sweeping force
Make its selection
Of the sand and shells alike
Leaving the discards
To weather and dry on the beach.

Life moves across
The gleaming grains of humanity
In much the same way.
Some are snatched for
A tumultuous ride
In the pounding surf,
Leaving others to weather,
Age
And . . .
Dry.

Their edges worn smooth.
Polished by rugged encounters
In the Sea of Life.
(Dottie Odell, used by permission)

Look for and come to appreciate those positive qualities, characteristics, and experiences that make you different from the crowd. Celebrate your individuality!

LOW LINERS

Some people hate themselves. Having critically examined their innermost selves, they conclude that no one as imperfect as they could be loved by anyone, not even themselves.

People who dislike themselves are immobilized by fears of being rejected. We call those people *low liners*. Their social involvements fall well below the dating relationship line on the Tally-Graph Model (see Figure 5-1).

Low liners are characterized by protective habits. They try to anticipate and prevent rejection by developing an elaborate defense strategy. In their eagerness to anticipate hurt, they often perceive rejection where there is none.

Cheri invited a casual friend to lunch one day, but she quickly withdrew her offer when she noticed a slight hesitancy in his response. Her friend, however, an open person, asked why she changed her mind. When she confessed to feeling that her offer was going to be rejected, he cautioned her, "Don't try to be a mind reader! The reason I hesitated is that I'm on a diet. I had to think of what I could eat if we went to the place you suggested. Then I remembered that the restaurant has a salad bar. I was

FIGURE 5-1

Portrait of a "Low Liner"

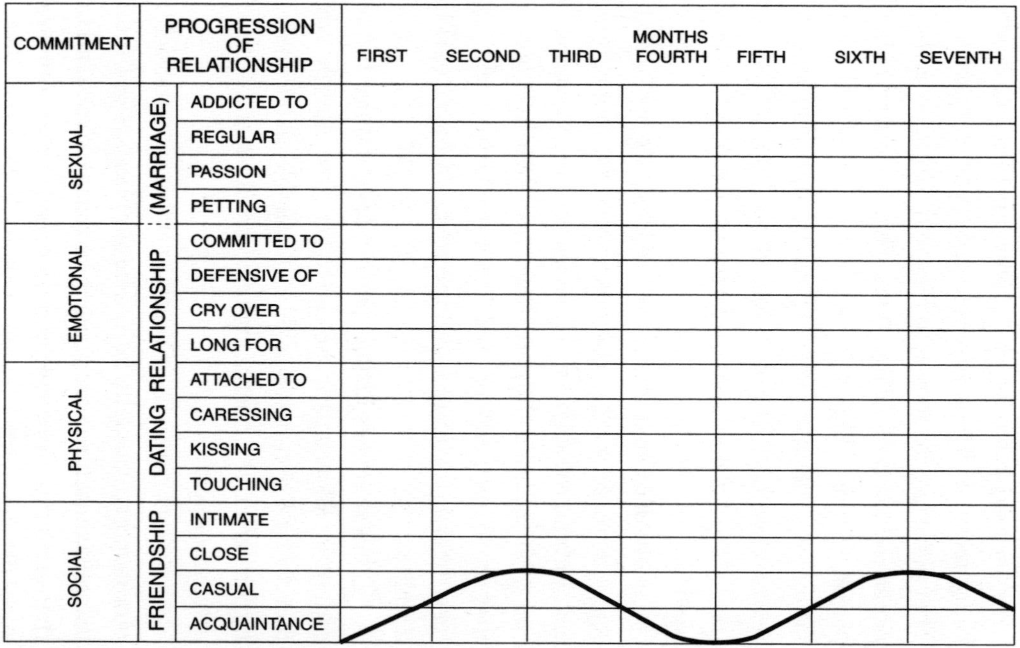

COMMITMENT	PROGRESSION OF RELATIONSHIP		MONTHS FIRST	SECOND	THIRD	FOURTH	FIFTH	SIXTH	SEVENTH
SEXUAL	(MARRIAGE)	ADDICTED TO							
		REGULAR							
		PASSION							
		PETTING							
EMOTIONAL	DATING RELATIONSHIP	COMMITTED TO							
		DEFENSIVE OF							
		CRY OVER							
		LONG FOR							
PHYSICAL		ATTACHED TO							
		CARESSING							
		KISSING							
		TOUCHING							
SOCIAL	FRIENDSHIP	INTIMATE							
		CLOSE							
		CASUAL							
		ACQUAINTANCE							

about to accept your invitation when you withdrew it. I really would like to have lunch with you!"

A second behavior of low liners is to reject others before being rejected. Their avoidance of social contact is obvious: They come late to group activities, and they leave early. They do not attend many social functions. Their attitude is either "These people wouldn't like me," or "I wouldn't like these people!" Either way, whether they are pathetically self-pitying or irritatingly snobbish, the result is loneliness. Ironically, their protective behavior causes them to be rejected, just as they feared they would be.

A third defense is self-centeredness. By applauding themselves, some people pretend not to need the affirmation of others. Without the slightest encouragement from you, they will tell you what successes they are, how great their lives are, and how they are so independent they do not need anyone else. Often we take them at their word, and the rejection they feared becomes a reality.

Other strategies include putting oneself down before others can, never allowing anyone else to get close enough to be a true friend whose rejection would be unbearable, deliberately becoming unattractive or behaving unbecomingly, and—the ultimate defense—suicide.

The terrible irony is that as elaborate as the defense system may be, it usually fails. The prophecy is self-fulfilling: If you tell yourself you are going to be rejected, you tend to be less than honest with people, and that results in eventual rejection after all!

Of course, the rejection experience is not limited to low liners. But all of us can cope with rejection if we put it in perspective. First, rejection of some fashion is inevitable. Not every person you reach out to is going to respond positively, just as you might not feel particularly attracted to every person you meet.

Next, recognize that sometimes your timing, not you, is the problem. Your telephone call to chat with a friend might have come at a bad time. The less-than-warm response you received might have had little to do with you personally.

When you sense rejection you need to determine what is actually being rejected—you or your invitation. A person struggling with a diet (as was Cheri's friend) may refuse any offers to share a meal or a snack but will respond eagerly to an invitation to go to a movie or to play tennis.

Even out-and-out rejection by another person does not indicate that no one will ever love you. And, of course, God loves you! As you find security in that fact, you should have fewer problems maintaining a healthy self-image.

SOURCES OF SELF-ESTEEM

A lack of self-acceptance may stem from *fear*, *guilt*, *unbelief*, or *unrealistic expectations*.

Some people have a *fear* of failure, rejection, discomfort, risk, the unknown, or embarrassment.

People may feel *guilty* about past failures, unconfessed sins, inadequacies, fears, procrastination, or negative emotions.

Other people may have a basic *unbelief* in their own worth, their abilities, a positive future, God's having a plan for their lives, or God's ability to effect miracles in their lives.

Finally, many people have *unrealistic expectations* of themselves and of others.

But how does one come to accept oneself? There are several foundations upon which self-esteem is based.

THE OPINION OF OTHERS

Basing your self-image on the opinion of others is attractive because it offers you the approval and affirmation of those who think well of you. But it also makes criticism a very difficult thing to handle, since criticism is often experienced as an attack on one's self-worth.

As a foundation for self-esteem, the opinions of others is as unstable as sand because (1) the perspective of others is not always correct; (2) people are not always honest with you about their opinions; (3) people's opinions are constantly changing to fit the societal norm; and (4) people do not always know the inner you, and so they are responding only to the public image you portray.

Consequently, although the opinions of others will contribute to a healthy self-concept, they cannot serve as a foundation for your entire structure.

ONE'S OWN OPINIONS

An alternative basis for being glad you are you is to depend only on your own internal approval. The advantage to this approach is the ability to be oblivious to the criticisms of others, having to answer only to yourself. However, there are also a few problems with this foundation: (1) You may have unrealistic expectations, which would result in a negative self-image if you failed to live up to them; (2) you might not be honest with yourself and simply deny the existence of whatever you cannot accept in yourself; (3) your opinion might be solely achievement- or accomplishment-oriented; failure to attain goals is perceived as indicative of personal inadequacy; (4) your opinions may be based on feelings rather than facts (accepting yourself on a day when you feel good is easy, but impossible on a "down" day).

Your personal opinion plays a part in having a positive self-image, but it is not consistent enough to serve as the base.

GOD'S OPINION

The only lasting foundation for a truly positive self-concept is God's opinion of you. Consider the following.

God already knows our innermost selves, our thoughts, desires, failings, secret vices, and futures. His view of us is realistic. In Psalm 139:1–6, David reminds us of this fact:

> O LORD, Thou hast searched me and known me.
> Thou dost know when I sit down and when I rise up;
> Thou dost understand my thought from afar.
> Thou dost scrutinize my path and my lying down,
> And art intimately acquainted with all my ways,
> Even before there is a word on my tongue,
> Behold, O LORD, Thou dost know it all.
> Thou hast enclosed me behind and before,
> And laid Thy hand upon me.
> Such knowledge is too wonderful for me;
> It is too high, I cannot attain to it.
>
> (NASB; see also Heb. 4:12–13)

God loved us enough, even in our sinful condition, to send His Son to redeem us and thereby make us acceptable to Him. Paul says, "But God demonstrates His own love toward us, in that while we were yet sinners, Christ died for us" (Rom. 5:8 NASB), and in Ephesians 1:6 we are told that "he hath made us accepted in the beloved" (KJV).

His love for us will not change, according to Romans 8:38–39, which says,

> For I am convinced that neither death, nor life, nor angels, nor principalities, nor things present, nor things to come, nor powers, nor height, nor depth, nor any other created thing, shall be able to separate us from the love of God, which is in Christ Jesus our Lord. (NASB; see also Jer. 31:3; Heb. 13:8)

God does not condemn us for our imperfections, unless we refuse to admit them. Instead, He is waiting to forgive us. First John 1:9 reads, "If we confess our sins, He is faithful and righteous to forgive us our sins and to cleanse us from all unrighteousness" (NASB; see also Rom. 8:1).

God wants us to accept His perspectives rather than our own.

> Oh, the depth of the riches both of the wisdom and knowledge of God! How unsearchable are His judgments and unfathomable His ways! For who has known the mind of the LORD, or who became His counselor? Or who has first given to Him that it might be paid back to him again? For from Him and through Him and to Him are all things. To Him be the glory forever. Amen. (Rom. 11:33–36 NASB; see also Isa. 55:8–9)

God wants us to be realistic, thinking neither too highly nor too negatively, about ourselves.

> For through the grace given to me I say to every man among you not to think or more highly of himself than he ought to think; but to think so as to have sound judgment, as God has allotted to each a measure of faith. (Rom. 12:3 NASB)

God is not finished with us! We as Christians are in the process of becoming spiritually mature. Paul reassures us that "He who began a good work in you will perfect it until the day of Christ Jesus" (Phil. 1:6 NASB).

So, the only sure foundation for a healthy and realistic self-image is God's Word.

YOU ARE GROWING

Learning self-acceptance may be a major obstacle in building a positive self-image, especially if nonacceptance has become a longtime habit. Perhaps the key is in fully understanding and accepting the fact that none of us are finished products! We are all in the process of become conformed to the image of Christ as we yield our lives as living sacrifices to the Lord.

THE AGE OF BECOMING

I have arrived at the age of becoming
No longer do I face the fear
Of what I shall be
When I grow up
I am becoming.
I see my armor chinks
For what they are—
Pressure points created by the stress of living.

Not permanent but changing.
I am becoming.
Relationships are not locked in—
But open,
Free to change
As life and time bring growth.
To each of us—
In different ways
We are becoming.
(Dottie Odell, used by permission)

In 1 John 3:1–2 we are reminded that imperfect as we are now, the Father has loved us enough to call us His children, and we will one day be like our Lord Jesus Christ Himself. But not until we see Him as He is—in heaven. For now, we are all in different stages of becoming conformed to His image.

The becoming process is sometimes slow and takes a lot of work. Sometimes we struggle as did Paul (see Rom. 7:15–25). Sometimes we fail. But when we do, we have an Advocate with the Father and the promise of forgiveness (see 1 John 1:9–2:2). And the victories are glorious as we recognize that we are more than conquerors through Him who loved us (see Rom. 8:37).

SHARE YOURSELF

Once you have learned to acknowledge and accept yourself as a unique, valuable, and growing individual, you can risk the vulnerability of sharing yourself with others. You can risk letting others get to know the real you. You can be authentic.

People will tend to respond to your honesty by becoming

more authentic themselves, because they can sense that you will be able to extend to them the same spirit of acceptance that you give yourself.

The level of communication between two authentic people increases because, as you accept and attempt to understand one another, you become less afraid of being judged, criticized, or rejected. Shallow, impersonal exchanges are discarded in favor of sharing ideas, emotions, struggles, and victories.

As dating partners, you will discover that as both persons develop self-esteem and interact openly with each other, the relationship will become more satisfyingly intimate.

6

ALIKE AND DIFFERENT

How many times have you heard a guy claim that he "will never understand girls"? Or have you ever seen a girl throw up her hands in exasperation, asking rhetorically, "Isn't that just like a guy?" Sometimes, particularly during periods of stress in a relationship, the opposite sex does seem to be impossible to understand.

In the last few years there has been a great deal of public and scientific interest in the subject of sex differences. Research has explored such possibilities as differences in the way female and male brain cells are used to solve problems, the effect of hormones on behavior, and culturally reinforced sex-role stereotyping. Few of the findings go unchallenged, so most conclusions are qualified meticulously rather than presented as absolute facts.

But whatever the cause, most people would agree that men and women *in general* seem to experience life differently. A friendship with a member of the same sex is somewhat different from a friendship with a person of the opposite sex. However, the specific differences between men and women (other than the obvious anatomy) are subject to debate, partly because no two individuals are exactly alike and because learned characteristics can be acquired by either sex.

PERSISTENT STEREOTYPES

If you and several of your friends each listed ten adjectives describing men and ten describing women, you probably would find a great number of similarities among the lists. This would happen partly because there exists a certain amount of cultural stereotyping and, within peer groups, a shared concept of the "ideal" girl or guy.

So it is important to discuss such differences when considering an intimate relationship with a member of the opposite sex. Otherwise, conflict that could be avoided will occur and, in some cases, even destroy a good relationship.

For discussion purposes, eighteen sets of characteristics are listed on the next page. List I includes characteristics generally ascribed to men, and List II is composed of words usually used to describe women. No guy is likely to have all the characteristics in List I; no girl is likely to have all of the characteristics in List II. Most people are a balance and blend of characteristics drawn from both lists.

UNDERSTANDING YOUR PARTNER

Let's explore some possible problems in relationships that are a result of not understanding a partner's approach to life situations.

ALIKE AND DIFFERENT

List I	List II
1. Provider for the home	1. Protector of the home
2. Initiator	2. Responder
3. Conquers by force or wit	3. Conquers with love
4. Objective	4. Subjective
5. Is thing-centered	5. Is people-oriented
6. Logical	6. Intuitive
7. Impersonal	7. Personal
8. Steady (Inflexible)	8. Adaptable
9. Communication is straight to the point	9. Communication is sensitive to the other person's responses
10. Looks for essentials	10. Looks for the aesthetic
11. Is future-minded (has long-range goals)	11. Is present-minded (sets short-range goals)
12. Needs significance in life	12. Needs security
13. Tendency to egotism	13. Tendency to jealousy
14. Soul-modest and body-free	14. Body-modest and soul-free
15. Desires sex	15. Dreams of love
16. Passionate	16. Romantic
17. Neglects tasks	17. Nags partner (often about neglecting tasks)
18. Defeated by discouragement	18. Defeated by loneliness

CASE #1. RAY / ONLY ONE WAY

Ray, a self-made businessman, has worked hard all of his life. He's never had time for "philosophizing about people," as he puts it. There's only one way to live, he claims: "You see a job that needs doing and you do it." He has little patience with anyone—man or woman—who isn't exactly like himself. Perhaps one reason Ray finds himself continuously dateless is that no one is ever going to be 100 percent like Ray!

Few people are as inflexible as Ray is, but often conflicts in relationships are the result of one partner's forgetting that there can be several different responses to a situation.

CASE #2. MOLLY / YOU'RE MY MAN

Molly's ideal man exhibits all eighteen of the characteristics in List I. She is upset when her date lacks even one of those characteristics. And if he should display a trait from List II, the relationship is over before it begins! Instead of relating to the specific person she is dating, Molly relates to all guys in exactly the same way, expecting them to conform to her ideal.

Your own list of male or female characteristics may be quite different from those in the two lists given. But whatever your concepts are, you can be sure of one thing: Your expectations have a lot to do with how you relate to your dating partner.

The bottom line is understanding that there are several different, and perfectly acceptable, ways to respond to a circumstance or situation. Just because a specific response is right for you doesn't mean it is the only right one. Discover those situations or issues to which you and your partner respond similarly. Identify your differences. What can you learn from one another's approach to life? How can you use your differences to make your partnership stronger? You each might take time also to describe what you expect in an ideal partner and affirm the ways in which your partner fits that description.

WORKING AT IT CAN BE FUN

Another way to learn more about your partner is to work together on projects or to plan "getting-to-know-you" activities. Below are several suggestions you may use.

1. DIGGING IN THE WORD. Find verses that have something to say about a specific topic (e.g., forgiveness, controlling the tongue, a quiet spirit, commitment, having fun, love). Then discuss what God says and how it applies to your relationship.

2. DIALOGUE. Plan a series of dialogues that will help you know each other better. A good resource for relevant subjects is John Powell's book *The Secret of Staying in Love* (Thomas More, 1995). On dates, or during telephone conversations, continue the dialogue until you have covered the areas on your list.

3. WORKBOOKS. Purchase one of the excellent resources on dating or marriage, and work through the assignments together. One such book is *Before You Say I Do*, by H. Norman Wright and Wes Roberts (Harvest House, 1997).

4. NEW ACTIVITIES. Make a list of twenty new activities or sports you have never tried together. Then experiment with them! Afterward discuss how much (or how little) each of you enjoyed the activity, and decide if you would like to do it again.

5. FINANCES. Discuss each other's spending habits. (a) Develop individual budgets for a month, and share your successes and failures. (b) Develop a budget for your dates and activities. Discuss each change, and agree together before any change is made. (c) Develop guidelines for sound financial management in

a marriage. (d) Share a funny experience involving your financial habits. (e) Share a "bad" experience you had involving money.

6. CLASS. Take a class together to learn something new, such as pottery making or swing dancing. Or participate in a book and movie discussion club.

7. DEVELOP A SKILL/KNOWLEDGE/ABILITIES (SKA) INVENTORY. List those SKAs you believe a person needs in order to function independently. Then evaluate each other (or yourself) to determine which of the SKAs are lacking. Next, develop a plan to acquire the needed SKAs, and follow through on the plan. Share your successes and struggles with the process of learning.

8. THIS IS MY LIFE. Have a "This Is My Life" night. Share stories, pictures, and mementos from your childhoods.

9. DO WORK PROJECTS TOGETHER. Try painting, building, organizing, writing, planning a party, or any other project together.

10. TEACHING. Share what you know by teaching one another a new skill.

11. COOKING/FOOD. Try cooking new dishes or tasting new foods. Go to several different restaurants or stores to sample different types of food and ethnic cuisine.

12. LETTERS. Write letters to each other once a week. Share ideas, thoughts, personal devotions, dreams, successes, or failures.

13. CONFLICT RESOLUTION. List twenty-five situations that commonly cause arguments or problems in a dating relationship, and discuss how you would be most likely to respond to each situation. Decide the most constructive and effective ways to respond to these situations, and plan how to ensure the use of effective approaches rather than destructive ones.

14. SHOPPING. Go shopping together and compare personal preferences in food, clothes, or home decorations.

15. GAMES. Play communication table games to improve your ease of conversation.

16. BOOKS. Read one or two books of common interest, and discuss your responses to the author's ideas.

17. COOPERATIVE SKILLS. Work on a team project to see if you can work with one another, resolving conflicts in a productive manner.

18. COMMUNITY INVOLVEMENT. Get involved in a community organization, program, or project for six months, and observe how well you each relate to others in a group.

The more you know about and understand your partner, the deeper you relationship will become. A sense of stability develops when you discover areas of predictability in the relationship. Also, the practice you gain in resolving conflicts will be of inestimable value if you and your partner marry.

7

Fairy Tales or Reality?

Just a few days before their wedding, Beth and Eric sat in their pastor's office discussing their feelings.

"We love each other so much and have been eagerly looking forward to getting married, totally confident that our marriage would never break up," Eric explained. "Then last week we found out that two of our best friends are getting a divorce. They've only been married a year!"

"Yes. And they seemed to love each other as much as Eric and I do," Beth broke in. "All of a sudden we realized it could happen to us too!"

Eric nodded in agreement.

By the end of the session, both Eric and Beth had voiced several concerns.

Eric

"Will she get irritated when we both have a bad day on the same day, and I don't seem to be very considerate because I'm too wrapped up in my own problems?

"Will I recognize during frustrating times, when singleness seems like something I should have clung to, that my frustration is clouding my perception?

"Will I remember that a fight, however ugly, doesn't mean that our love has died, but rather that we both have some growing up to do?

"Will we continue to give each other the freedom and encouragement to grow as we do now?

"Will we continue to care and share and build together out of eager love, without the process turning out to be just hard work?"

BETH

"Will he really understand when all of my deadlines come due at once, and I'm not coping very well? Will he accept that something has to give temporarily and that it might be spending time with him?

"Will I accept his taking a walk to cool off after a fight without feeling rejected or deserted?

"Will I, after years of developing the ability to be independent and to solve my own problems, be able to consider Eric's needs, ideas, and suggestions as important as my own?

"Will he understand that my independence is a habit and not a deliberate affront to him?

"Will we continue to keep God at the center of our relationship or will we go off on our own and fail?"

What Eric and Beth are saying is that they have a lot of expectations about what a committed relationship should be. Most of us have similar ideas.

UNLIMITED EXPECTATIONS

What we must ascertain is if our expectations have been carefully considered and based in reality. All of us have certain expectations of a loving, committed relationship based on our perceptions of what that interaction should be like. Our expectations tend to become more numerous and significant as the relationship becomes more serious. For example, Mandy would be mildly disappointed if a friend were to forget her birthday, but she would be deeply crushed if Alex, her dating partner, were to do the same. In fact, Alex is expected not only to send flowers but also to bring a gift and to take her out to dinner. Since Alex agrees with Mandy's ideas for celebrating her birthday, and she reciprocates on his special day, they have no problems in this instance.

Expectations that are realistic, discussed with, accepted by, or negotiated with a partner, help strengthen and stabilize relationships between dating couples.

However, sometimes our expectations in a relationship are little more than romantic fantasies. We seem to believe those hundreds of romantic movies, which depict the familiar myth of Prince Charming and the beautiful maiden who live happily ever after. We want to be like the silver-screen lovers who, overcoming seemingly impossible obstacles to reach each other's arms, achieve perfect happiness just before the movie credits roll.

UNREALISTIC EXPECTATIONS DESTROY RELATIONSHIPS

Few relationships can survive if one or both partners cling to unrealistic expectations.

Unrealistic Expectations Result in a Critical Attitude

Because no one is perfect, the partner always falls short of the expectations and therefore will be criticized and made to feel inadequate. What affirmation is given always seems to end with a "but . . ." For example, "You look lovely, *but* I wish you could be ready on time! We're fifteen minutes late already!"

Unrealistic Expectations Preclude Having an Accepting Attitude

Helen's ex-husband's incurable procrastination was particularly irritating to her organized, do-it-now nature during the two years of their relationship. After their divorce, Helen started dating other guys; but if she discovered the slightest hint of procrastination in him, she couldn't even enjoy the date! She now realizes that her negative over-reaction to this quality must be carefully unlearned, since almost any guy she meets occasionally puts off doing certain tasks.

Most of us similarly overreact to specific traits or situations because of past hurts—which we've promised ourselves not to suffer again. We need to learn that healing comes not just from avoiding similar experiences but also by forgiving those who have hurt us. Only when we have learned to forgive can we be truly whole and free to develop serious, lasting relationships.

People are not completed projects. They are always in the process of developing, but the process is stifled in a nonaccepting atmosphere. Also, people having unrealistic expectations of a partner will tend to view a partner's progress as something long overdue, rather than as a cause for joint celebration.

UNREALISTIC EXPECTATIONS ARE UNFAIR

Expecting a partner to live up to an unrealistic ideal when we ourselves are still imperfect is the height of injustice!

Yet, still we dream. Paul, orphaned at birth, rejected by the other children in the foster home where he was raised, and never having had a trusting, open, and caring relationship with another person, has an understandable expectation. He wants one person all to himself who will care for him, believe in and affirm his efforts, love and cherish him, and most important, always be available for him when he needs her. He doesn't think that is too much to ask.

Sorry, Paul, it is. Expecting another human being to always be available (physically, emotionally, psychologically, or spiritually) to another is not only a burden but also an impossibility. While there will be periods of idealistic compatibility, each person has individual needs, energy cycles, and desires that will not always match a partner's. People are individuals, not duplicates. Neither are they interlocking puzzle pieces with opposing highs and lows for perfect dovetailing in a relationship.

UNREALISTIC EXPECTATIONS LEAD TO LONELINESS

Having unrealistic expectations is not the problem. Refusing to relinquish them is! For in clinging to a fantasy, one must inevitably reject every possible partner and, therefore, end up alone and lonely.

Even establishing close friendships is difficult for a person who refuses to accept people as they are. We all need interaction, creative and loving conflict resolution, affirmation and feedback, especially from close friends. But people who expect perfection in others cannot be or have an open friend. Therefore, their personal growth is stunted.

IDENTIFYING UNREALISTIC EXPECTATIONS

"But I don't expect perfection," Brad argues. "I only want what any guy wants from a woman. I want Carla to be thoughtful when I'm tired and understanding when I have to work late. I've told her that several times, but she just doesn't listen."

Actually Brad has two problems. First, few people have the same expectations in a relationship, and second, he has never defined his expectations to Carla in terms of specific actions.

When Brad works late, she tries to be understanding by preparing a late supper for him, offering lots of sympathy and attention, while asking dozens of solicitous questions about the events of the day.

Brad feels hassled. He would prefer that Carla cancel their date, allow him to go home to bed without any long conversations on the phone, and not call him early the next morning. In this situation, Brad's basic expectation may be perfectly reasonable, but his expecting Carla to know what he means without being specific is unrealistic.

Perhaps you, too, have been guilty of acting as if you and your partner are mind readers. Take time to check out what you think your partner wants from you and to explain specifically what you desire in your relationship.

Most people who are serious about a relationship are willing to keep their expectations within realistic bounds. The problem is, often we are not aware of having unrealistic expectations. If we could go to a Web site, click a button, and receive a printout of our expectations in a partner, we might find it easier to identify potential problem areas. Unfortunately, no such site exists. So, we are left to discuss those expectations we are cognizant of and to deal with the rest as problems arise.

Often we can identify unmet expectations when we experience negative emotions toward our partners. For example:

DISAPPOINTMENT

SAYING: "I'm so disappointed we didn't go to see the Van Gogh exhibit when it was in town."

CAN MEAN: "We had discussed going, and he had promised to get tickets for one of the shows. So I expected him to follow through."

OR: "I didn't say anything about wanting to go, but I expected him to know I'd like to do something like that."

ANGER

SAYING: "She had no right to invite another couple to double date without asking me first!"

CAN MEAN: "Since we have an agreement to consult each other on these types of decisions, she broke our agreement."

OR: "I expected her to want to be alone with me tonight. If I don't need anyone else, why should she?"

RESENTMENT

SAYING: "He spends all of his extra money on his nieces, yet we can't even afford to eat out once a month!"

CAN MEAN: "I expect him to be as generous with me as he is with others."

OR: "I'd really like him to forget those kids ever existed!"

FRUSTRATION

SAYING: "She spends so much time talking on her cell phone with friends that sometimes I have to try five or six times before I can reach her."

CAN MEAN: "I expect to be more important to her than any of her friends."

OR: "I expect her to be available to me whenever I want to talk with her."

TAKE THE HINT

The alternative to having unrealistic expectations is to accept and deal with reality. The price is giving up dreams; the payoff is personal growth and the opportunity to develop wonderful and supportive relationships, not only with friends but also with a dating partner.

As you can see by the above examples, negative feelings are sometimes red flags signaling unrealistic expectations. So, whenever you experience negative feelings toward your partner, take that opportunity to investigate what's behind the emotions.

Realistic expectations can be discussed and possibly met. If the unmet expectation is realistic within the framework of the relationship, then you can share your feelings with your partner and work through the issues to an acceptable resolution. When sharing negative feelings, the statements must never be accusatory:

"You hurt me!"

Rather, they should share information while retaining the responsibility for the feeling:

"When you do _____________, I feel_____________."

It is important to note that expressing negative feelings in no way obligates the listener to change behavior. Change is always a choice. However, often people will respond to the expression of negative feelings by explaining their perspectives of, or reasons for, their behavior in such a way that the hurt is eliminated through understanding. And many times the explanation is coupled with a promise to change so the partner won't be hurt in the future.

Unrealistic expectations can be discarded. If you discover by examining negative feelings toward a partner that you are harboring unrealistic expectations, you can choose to let go of them and free yourself (and your partner) of future pain relating to unmet, unrealistic expectations.

ASK QUESTIONS

One survey of Christian men and women resulted in the following lists of expectations in a partner. Do you agree with these characteristics? Does your partner? Spend an evening or two discussing the lists, explaining and exploring the specific behaviors you do find desirable in a lifelong mate.

According to the girls surveyed, the ideal guy would be

- Committed to putting Christ first in his life, grounded in the Word, and a spiritual leader. Church attendance and Christian service would be a vital part of his life.
- Able to lead. Making good decisions and taking responsibility for following up on plans are important, but most women also stated a true preference for participative leadership in a marriage partner.
- Affectionate and loving. He would both talk of and show his love.
- In control of himself. An unbridled temper or tongue, a tendency toward physical violence, and financial irresponsibility were listed as reasons girls lose respect for a guy. He would also be in control of his sexual desires and moral choices.
- Masculine. Most girls want guys to have more of the characteristics in List I than those in List II in Chapter 6.
- Tender and considerate. Sensitivity to the feelings of others and being unafraid to reach out and open up on an emotional level ranked high on the lists.
- Attractive.

According to the guys surveyed, the ideal girl would be

- Committed to putting Christ first in her life and the relationship. Her personal relationship with God would be strong and close. She would be actively involved in the church.
- Submissive. *Submission* has been defined as "voluntary cooperation with another's leadership."
- Responsive, loving, and affectionate. The guys wanted women to respond to their love and, as wives, to be enthusiastic sexual partners.
- Supportive. Men cited a desire for support when making decisions, when succeeding, or when failing miserably. Criticizing, nagging, complaining, and belittling were given as easy ways to destroy a relationship.
- Feminine. Most guys wanted girls to have more of the characteristics from List II than from List I in Chapter 6.
- Gentle in spirit. It was mentioned that many women, who would never be physically violent, harbor hearts full of hatred and bitterness. These men wanted women to be in control of their emotional lives and honest enough about negative emotions to confront their partners lovingly.
- Attractive.

DARING TO BE HONEST

As you become honest and open in your relationship to the point of sharing what you want most, you will experience a tremendous surge of freedom. Gone are the fears of inadvertently offending your partner. Frustrating attempts to second-guess what is expected become unnecessary. Mutual trust and confidence grow because you each know where you stand with the other. And with the increase in the degree of openness comes a commensurate rise in the level of intimacy.

Once in a while dating partners who begin to be honest with one another discover that they have serious differences in expectations. Yet neither person is willing to yield or change in any way. In such situations, if the people truly cannot accept their partners or negotiate their differences, their only responsible choice is to withdraw from the intimacy of a dating relationship and return to a friendship level, for to continue on together is only to hurt one another eventually.

Letting go of a dating relationship, even an unsatisfactory one, can be very scary, because sometimes our fears get in the way. We become convinced we will never find another partner. We fear being forever alone and lonely. We're afraid we will later regret our decision to end the relationship. Consequently, instead of facing squarely who we are and how we respond to our partners, we sometimes start making *unasked for* sacrifices. Of course, somewhere in the back of our minds is the idea that these self-denials will be repaid with interest. Soon, though, the relationship is out of balance and one-sided, and the unacknowledged debt grows.

The most frequent result is an angry parting and the death of the relationship when the giving partner either becomes a "non-person" or decides to demand a turn at being the receiver.

Nancy and Tom had this problem. For the three months they had been dating, Nancy had always let Tom choose what they should do and where they should go on their dates. Because she enjoyed his company, she didn't even mind going places she wouldn't have enjoyed without him. The pleasure of *just being together* seemed enough. So she watched sports on television, went to science-fiction movies, ate Chinese food at least once a week, and listened for hours while he talked about his job, his interests, and his plans. Tom always knew what he wanted or what he thought about something, so Nancy rarely voiced her opinion or made a suggestion. Even when he was a couple of hours late for dinner at her house (without calling to let her know) or when he embarrassed her by teasing her in public, she wouldn't say a word.

Nancy never told Tom that she longed to share her feelings and ideas with him, or that she sometimes felt that he didn't truly love her because of his thoughtlessness. Her tears of hurt and resentment were shed in the privacy of her own bedroom. She often wished, however, that Tom would repay her devotion by doing things her way or by going out of his way to please her once in a while.

At first Tom thought he had found the perfect mate. They apparently shared the same tastes and ideas about life. But after a few more months, he began to feel that he was carrying the responsibility for the whole relationship since he had to make all of the decisions. Nancy never seemed to take the initiative; in fact, now that he thought about it, she was almost boring!

One night Tom tried to explain his concerns to Nancy. He asked her to be a little more assertive and to contribute more of herself to the relationship. Well, Nancy took him at his word and started expressing her dislike of watching sports every evening and her preference for going out every once in a while. Her favorite foods were Italian and French. The more she opened up, the less, Tom realized, they had in common. A very surprised guy, he decided to break off the relationship.

Nancy was angry, bewildered, and hurt. And yet, she had set up the situation by not being honest with Tom from the beginning. She had led Tom to believe that she was the person she had pretended to be. Although Nancy might have been able to continue the relationship with Tom a little longer if she had not been open, the end result would have been the same.

Although it may be painful to be open and honest, it is more painful in the long run not to be!

Being honest allows the relationship to have balance, to include both giving to and taking from one's partner, to involve workable compromises and problem resolutions in which both partners are satisfied. Being honest prevents the buildup of resentment and bitterness.

IT TAKES TIME

Spending time together constructively as discussed in Chapter 3 and being open about feelings and expectations are important ways to build lasting relationships, without any destructive games. The early stages of relationships are the times to start sharing ideas, opinions, lifestyles, dreams, preferences, and feelings, so you truly get to know each other rather than making assumptions.

Of course, the learning process is never complete, because

people are always changing as they strive to become the person and partner God expects them to be.

Adjusting to the personality of another person is a long process. You must decide what life changes you are willing to make and then practice the appropriate new behaviors. Although there may seem to be instant trust, love, and compatibility between two people, the reliability of first impressions must be verified over a period of time. If trust or love is assumed too quickly, there is no real foundation. Then, when trouble comes and the trust is broken or the love ignored, the total relationship can be abandoned too easily. On the other hand, if trust has been built up through many experiences, it can survive attacks and problems.

As you strive for openness and acceptance and survive the test of time, you will realize the substance of reality will far surpass any unrealistic dreams.

8

BUILDING TOGETHER

The warm fire blazing in the retreat lodge fireplace allowed the group inside to ignore the cold rain outside. After spending the morning in workshops and the afternoon hiking through the mountains, the four couples were happy just to sit around the fire, drink coffee, and talk.

"Successful Christian Dating Relationships" was the theme of the weekend retreat, so quite naturally the conversation eventually circled back to the topic of that morning's workshop: "Setting and Reaching Goals."

"Have you and Sharon talked about any long-range goals as a couple?" Richard asked Nate, starting a lengthy discussion during which each of the couples shared their goals. Some of these included

- building a mountain cabin
- moving to California and getting better jobs
- taking turns putting each other through college

- traveling as much as possible
- getting married in a few months and making the relationship work
- eventually owning their own home

Short-range goals usually involved such practicalities as

- finishing this semester of college
- getting a summer job
- setting a wedding date

WHY SET GOALS?

Goal setting is important in a person's life because it contributes to a positive self-concept. So every individual will want to identify and plan to achieve goals. The process of setting goals helps a person identify and abandon unrealistic expectations of themselves. Further-more, goals provide direction and purpose and, therefore, are a great deterrent to boredom and depression. Reaching goals provides a sense of accomplishment, satisfaction, and confidence.

Logically, then, the process of setting and working toward goals is very important for two people who are working at developing an intimate, lasting relationship. Working through the goal setting and planning process helps the couple begin to identify and discuss their expectations in terms of specific behaviors. As expectations are clarified, they can be agreed to, negotiated, or worked through. Hopefully, unrealistic expectations will be modified or discarded.

As the various shared goals are identified and listed in order of importance, a couple begins to agree on the direction their relationship will take. Discussing differences in the relative importance of the goals or values involved provides opportunities to understand one another better, to practice resolving conflicts, and to invest in the relationship. The shared satisfaction of reaching a mutual goal increases the intimacy and level of commitment to the partnership.

Partners who are committed to a relationship will want to have not only mutual goals but also individual objectives that require the encouragement and even the assistance of both partners.

CHOOSING GOALS

Sometimes the goals we set have to do with the process of living in general: earning a living, acquiring possessions, accomplishing tasks, or learning better skills. However, when focusing on becoming a better partner in a relationship, you might consider the following:

- What characteristics do I need to develop?
- What communication skills do I lack?
- What practical skills do I need to learn (e.g., balancing a budget or caring for a car)?

Mutual goals might be set for such things as

- the amount of time spent alone together during the month

- the level of emotional intimacy of the relationship
- ways of keeping the relationship under control
- ways of being accountable for controlling the relationship
- whether or not to go to a counselor and, if so, for how long
- how time together will be spent
- how much time apart will be spent on activities that involve the partner (phone calls or e-mailing)
- how to get to know where the partner is in his or her personal growth
- when and how to discuss each other's expectations of the partner and the relationship
- learning what is unique and special about each other
- how conflicts will be resolved
- how and when negative feelings will be discussed

These are all important areas for goal setting, but as Christians we have an additional goal to consider—God's will and plan for our lives.

In setting individual goals, therefore, we need to consider the following questions:

- What is the overall purpose of my life?
- What spiritual gift(s) do I have, and how can I use it (them) for His glory?

- What Christlike characteristics are missing from or underdeveloped in my life?
- What is my commitment to the local community of believers?
- How can my life better glorify God and serve as a witness to His power?

In addition to assisting one another to develop individual objectives, you will want to evaluate your relationship in light of biblical standards for true love.

Once you have developed a comprehensive list of goals for your relationship (as well as personal goals for each of you), the next step is to assign priorities to those goals. To work on only two or three top-priority objectives at one time is wise if success is to be achieved within a reasonably short period of time.

DEVELOPING SPECIFIC GOALS

For the goal-setting process to be successful, goals must be reachable, measurable, dated, and written.

REACHABLE

A goal must be something that can be reached within the time frame set to work toward it. Everyone has a few big dreams, but actual goals must be realistic. Whatever it takes to reach a goal must be within the control of the individual.

MEASURABLE

When goals are stated in general, nonmeasurable terms, there is no conscious awareness of when goals have been reached. Goals that are useful must be stated in specific terms. "Measurable" means specifying how many, how often, how long, how much, or exactly what will be accomplished if the goal is met. The test of a goal's measurability is whether you answer yes or no within the time frame. For instance, "Becoming a better person" is not easily measurable, but "In order to be a better person, I will read one self-help book a month," this is a goal to which you can answer, "yes, I did" or "no, I didn't." That is what measurability is all about.

Dated

Open-ended goals are of little value. You will need to establish a time frame during which you will reach your goals. Of course, the dates must be reasonable and may be changed if an unexpected circumstance occurs. However, careful consideration should be given to modifying time frames; if they are too easily changed, they become meaningless.

Time frames may be phrased in terms of (a) starting dates for an ongoing goal or (b) completion dates for actions or projects.

When setting time frames, it is best to concentrate on goals that can be accomplished in three months or less. This allows for frequent reinforcement of efforts expended. A goal that is too long term (reading the Bible twenty minutes a day for the rest of your life) has no provision for achievement, because the goal is not achieved until the person's life is over! Ongoing goals can be reset every three months. When setting goal dates, use completion dates for a project (cleaning the garage, painting the apartment) and beginning dates for the process (exercising three times a week). Process goal dates need to include periodic evaluation time frames to ensure that the process continues to be important.

WRITTEN

Since the best plans in the world are worthless unless they are implemented, accountability in the form of written goals is needed. The act of stating your plans on paper makes them visible and provides a way of reminding you on what to focus. (An example of a goal-setting form is given at the end of this chapter.)

If we do not set completion dates or discipline ourselves to follow through on plans, we often have several half-finished projects. Without a written reminder, we often procrastinate so long that we never get around to working on objectives.

FOLLOW THROUGH

Setting goals is a meaningless exercise unless the plans are implemented. If, in spite of the fact that the goal has been written and that it fulfills all of the above criteria for an appropriate goal, there is a reluctance to start the project or that it has been impossible to complete the goal on time, further evaluation is needed. People who hesitate before beginning a project may be afraid of failing, or they may discover that this project isn't one of their top priorities after all, even if they *think it should be*. When completion dates can't be reached despite sincere efforts, then perhaps the goal was too ambitious for the period assigned. A long-range, complex objective is best divided into smaller, reasonable steps with intermediate time frames so that success can be affirmed at each step.

CELEBRATE SUCCESS

Each time you and your dating partner achieve a goal, affirm one another and celebrate your success. Discuss what impact this achievement has on your relationship. Share your feelings about the steps you took and the eventual accomplishment. Talk about the next goals you will be working on together . . . and watch as your relationship becomes closer than ever before.

GOAL SETTING

The purpose of life for the Christian is to *glorify God* and to *enjoy Him forever.* This clearly points the direction our new lives in Christ are to take, but we need *goals* to help us accomplish this challenging purpose.

A goal is a future event that can be accomplished in a given time and by which our progress can be measured. We need goals to help us arrive at what God wants us to be and to help us accomplish what we set out to do. For our life's purpose to become reality, we must make long-range, short-range, and immediate goals.

IMMEDIATE	SHORT-RANGE	LONG-RANGE	LIFE PURPOSE
Now	Next year	5 years	15–20 years

In order to set godly goals, we must understand our relationship to the Lord Jesus, the community of believers, and the work of Christ. Commitment to Jesus as Lord is the foundation we build on as we pursue our life purposes. Our commitment to the community of believers, His Body, makes possible our growth to maturity, and commitment to the work of Christ ensures us of a fulfilling life goal.

GOAL PLANNING

1. Do you have a life goal? What is it?
2. What do you believe God wants you to be or to have accomplished fifteen to twenty years from now?
3. In reaching toward your goal, describe what progress you would like to make by five years from now.
4. What practical short-range goals should you plan to accomplish this year toward your life goal?
5. List those goals that require another's cooperation. Example: "Improvement in my dating relationship."

Goals should be measurable. You should be able to give a yes or no answer as to whether they have been attained.

BUILDING TOGETHER				
	PERSONAL	FAMILY	JOB	MINISTRY
IMMEDIATELY BY__ /__ /__				
NEXT MONTH BY__ /__ /__				
IN 3 MONTHS BY__ /__ /__				
IN 6 MONTHS BY__ /__ /__				
IN 1 YEAR BY__ /__ /__				
IN 2 YEARS BY__ /__ /__				

6. What goals have you accomplished this past year?

1 – 3 MONTHS				
4 – 6 MONTHS				
7 – 9 MONTHS				
10 – 12 MONTHS				

9

AVOIDING THE PITFALLS

Because developing an intimate relationship with a member of the opposite sex is one of the more exciting and satisfying experiences in life, it is sometimes difficult to spread the intimacy-building activities over a sufficiently long period of time for the relationship to develop real depth. There is a temptation to rush into commitment, to speed up the progression, and to spend as much time together as possible right away.

Using the Talley-Graph Model once again, let's look at the consequences of going too fast in a relationship.

A NATURAL PROGRESSION

Janet and Matt started dating in January and by March had decided to become more than intimate friends. Although their time alone together accumulated only slightly faster than the ideal curve (see Figure 9-1), they did cross over into a sexual relationship about a month prior to getting married.

FIGURE 9-1

The Development of a Natural Relationship

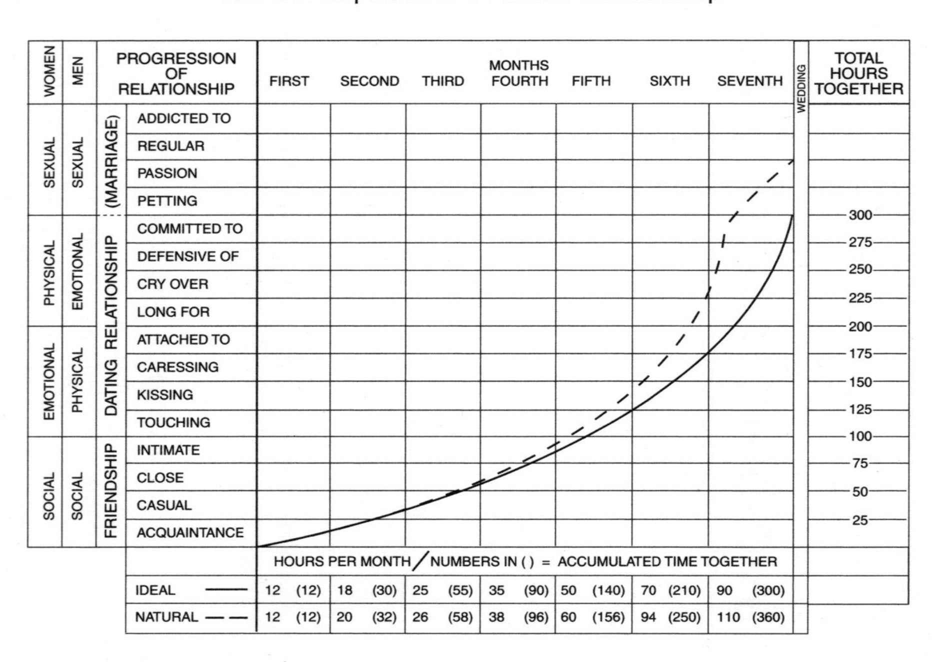

FIGURE 9-2

The Development of a Sensual Relationship

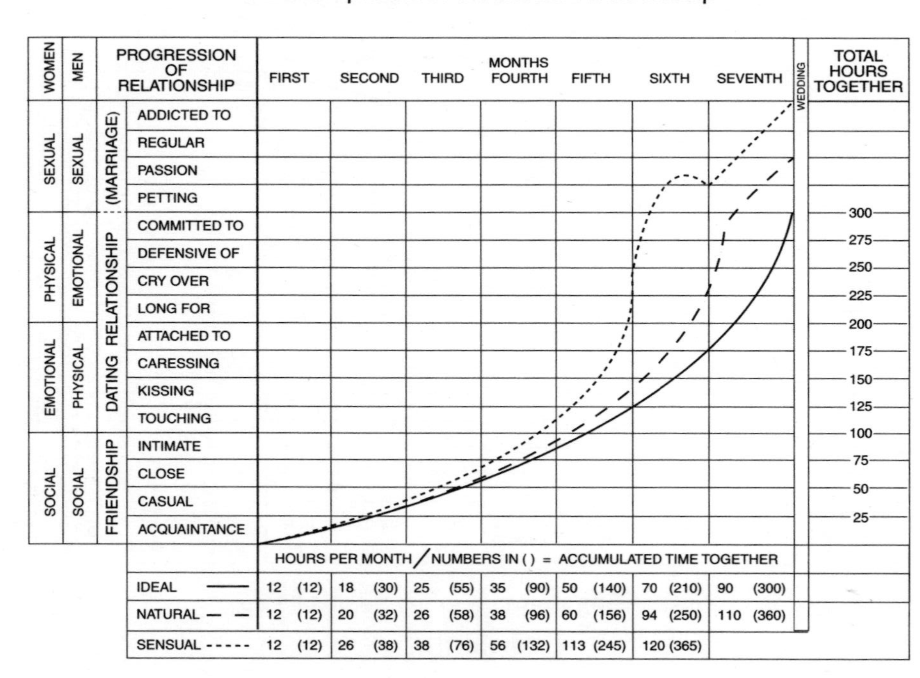

FIGURE 9-3

The Development of a Lustful Relationship

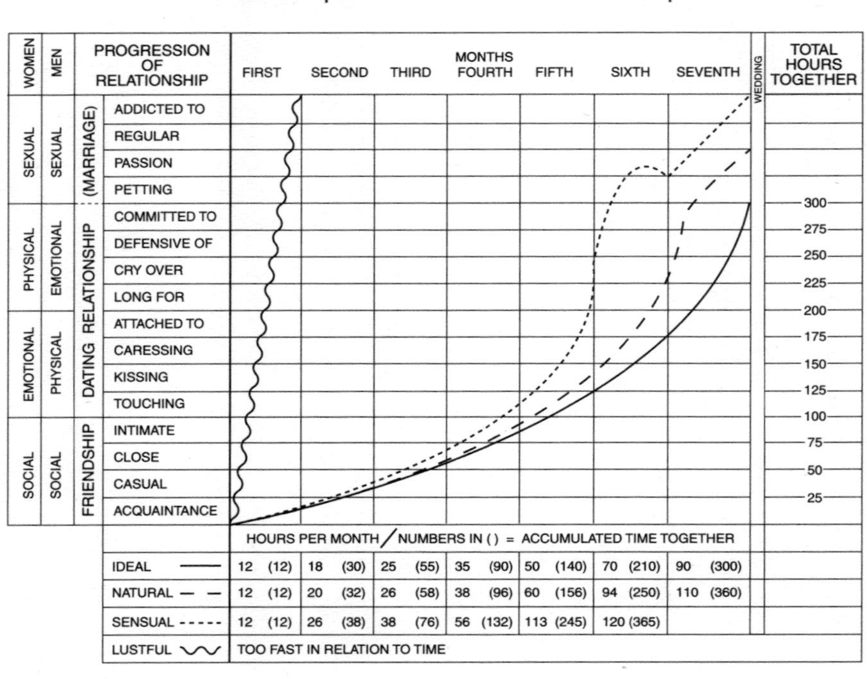

A SENSUAL PROGRESSION

Dinah and Nathan's relationship started out much like Janet and Matt's, except that after three months of dating they significantly increased the time they spent alone together. As you can see by Figure 9-2, they started heavy petting shortly after their fifth month of dating. For about a week, they tried to let things cool off; but because they continued spending long evenings together, they soon not only went to bed together but began sleeping together regularly.

A LUSTFUL PROGRESSION

Sharri and William started dating, went to bed, and moved in together within five weeks after having met. They actually knew very little about one another and hadn't had time to build much of a relationship. Theirs was merely a convenient union based on physical attraction and emotional excitement, rather than a permanent commitment based on friendship (see Figure 9-3).

SO, WHAT'S THE PROBLEM?

"I may get hurt later on," Dinah admits candidly, "but for right now I'm going to enjoy what I have with Nathan!"

Dinah's prophecy will come true; she will be hurt by the relationship. And Nathan will be also, for that matter! That's the problem with letting the progression of a relationship get out of control, as all three of the couples mentioned have.

PROBLEMS WITH NATURAL AND SENSUAL PROGRESSIONS

Because these two types of relationships move quickly from the casual stage of friendship to physical and emotional intimacy, there is a strong possibility that the skills required for maintaining intimacy at each level were not fully developed. Yet, these are the very skills that become the most significant in a lifelong marriage. Getting married without these skills is a little like attempting to climb Mt. Everest after taking only one weekend course in mountain climbing!

A second problem is that relationships need to be developed over a sufficient period of time for the romantic fantasy to give way to a joyous reality. However, a rapid acceleration of the relationship makes it so exciting that the romantic dream is kept alive just when it should be fading away. In other words, when a couple make an emotional commitment to one another, there is the initial thrill of belonging to someone special, of being "a twosome," of having someone to care for, and of discovering each other's personal preferences. Only after that initial novelty wears off will you be able to discover if you actually do enjoy these things and want to make a lifelong commitment to each other. A couple, who allows their relationship to accelerate faster than the ideal curve will be living a romantic fantasy (eromania) rather than practicing realistic love and commitment (see Figure 9-4).

A third problem is that, although developing sexual intimacy is more fun and less work than developing intimacy at the emotional, physical, and friendship levels, sex without intimacy at those levels is not truly intimate. Thus the most beautiful intimacy God planned for us is reduced to a meaningless biological exercise.

More important, there is the factor of having violated God's rules for moral behavior, which in turn causes a break in our fellowship with the Father.

The question is how far will you go, and when do you choose

to get out of the relationship rather than get to 10? Be honest about the physical part of the relationship. Circle the number that represents the extent of your physical involvement.

1 Look

2 Touch

3 Lightly holding hands

4 Constantly holding hands

5 Light kiss

6 Strong kiss

7 French kiss

****

8 Fondling breasts

9 Fondling sexual organs

10 Sexual intercourse

Going beyond 7 prior to marriage will damage your spiritual lives and your moral characters.

PROBLEMS WITH A LUSTFUL PROGRESSION

Some relationships progress so quickly that there is no curve on our graph, only a straight line upward.

First, the problems already mentioned are magnified. For example, instead of the relational skills just being underdeveloped, they probably do not even exist. Instead of a commitment based on romance, there is probably no commitment

FIGURE 9-4

The Line Between Eromania and Reality

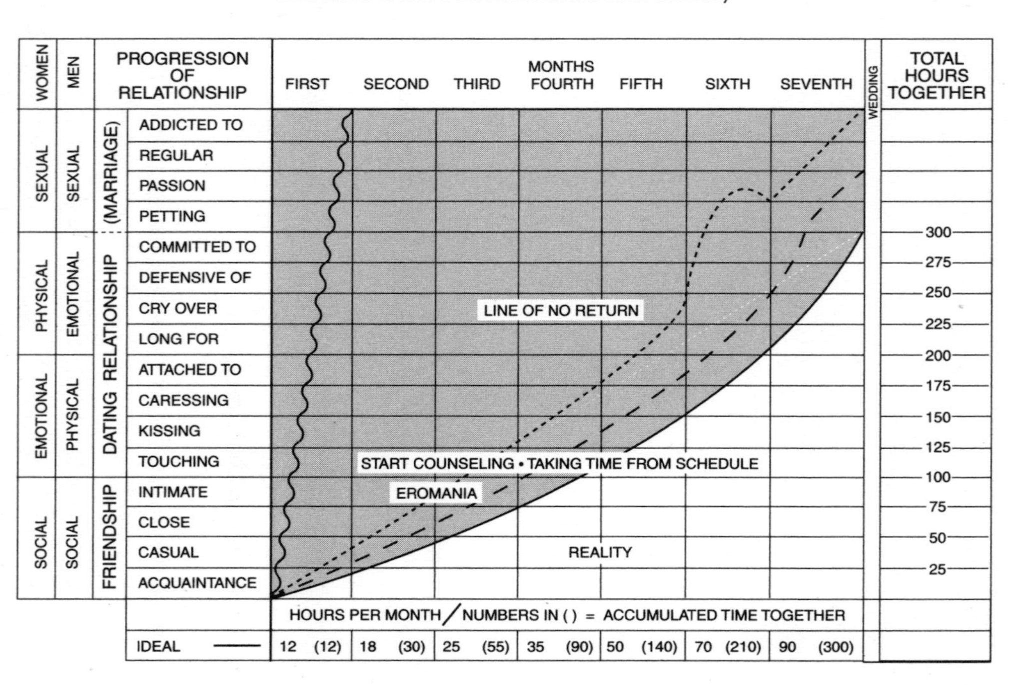

at all. Genuine communication is probably minimal. Confrontations or arguments will tend to be "resolved" in the bedroom. The lack of depth in the relationship allows it to break up easily at the first hint of serious differences between the couple.

Second, should the couple decide to back off from their sexual relationship, they would most likely return to the level of mere acquaintances because the friendship level was never developed.

A third problem is that people tend to develop new relationships based on prior experiences. Consequently, those whose patterns have been to become sexually intimate quickly will tend to repeat those patterns over and over, getting involved with one partner after another. Unless they make a deliberate choice to approach relationships differently, they will spend their entire lives hurting and being hurt as relationship after relationship breaks off.

So, the underlying problem with all three of the less-than-ideal progressions illustrated is that the end goal—a strong, lasting relationship—becomes less and less of a real possibility because the initial structure is weak. *True friendship is the safety net under a marriage*. Marriage can be like walking on a high wire: Sooner or later you are going to have a conflict and fall off the wire of intimacy. That is when you desperately need the safety net of friendship. God knew what He was doing when He instructed us to wait until after marriage to explore sexual intimacy.

THE MESSAGE IS LOVE

God has provided instructions for successful living, even though people have rarely understood the "whys" behind His rules. So, from the beginning, God's rules have been disobeyed by rebellious human beings who usually seem surprised at the adverse consequences of their behaviors.

In the books of the Law, God gave the Israelites strict instructions as to what they could and couldn't eat. Often these rules seem unreasonably restrictive, yet scientists have determined that those laws were nutritionally sound for a tribe of people living in the desert with no refrigeration and unsophisticated sanitary practices. The laws were given so that the Israelites would enjoy good health. The same principle was behind God's instruction for coping with diseased persons who might infect others.

Time after time God instructed His people to obey Him, despite their natural instincts. Success always followed obedience (recall the wall of Jericho and Gideon's victory). Disobedience brought defeat (the battle of Ai and the captivity of Israel). We can read hundreds of stories in the Old Testament that illustrate these principles, yet the Israelites never really learned to choose obedience over rebellion consistently. And so God had their stories written for us in order that we might learn from their mistakes (see 1 Cor. 10:11–13).

In spite of all of this, obedience today is still a difficult choice for some of us at times.

LOVE IS THE KEY WORD

God didn't sit up in heaven and decide to make life difficult for us by forbidding us to do certain things. He didn't set up an obstacle course we have to run in order to prove our love for Him. Each law God gives is designed to assist us in reaching our highest potential and in living the abundant life. When people fail to follow God's standard, they experience the consequences: impaired functioning, broken relationships, failures, and sometimes even personal injury.

In the same way that it hurts parents when their children suffer for wrong choices (such as contracting an STD after sexual promiscuity), it hurts God when we make wrong choices. During His stay on earth, Christ emphasized the Father-child relationship we have with God. In Matthew 7:7–12 Christ encourages the disciples to recognize just how much God wants us to have a good life. He says, "If you, then, though you are evil, know how to give good gifts to your children, how much more will your Father in heaven give good gifts to those who ask him!" (v. 11 NIV).

His plans for us are always referred to as perfect. Paul urges, "Offer your bodies as living sacrifices, holy and pleasing to God—this is your spiritual act of worship. Do not conform any longer to the pattern of this world, but be transformed by the renewing of your mind. Then you will be able to test and approve what God's will is—his good, pleasing and *perfect* will" (Rom. 12:1–2 NIV, italics added).

BUT SEX IS MY OWN AFFAIR!

"I don't see why God is so interested in what I do in the privacy of my own bedroom!" Kevin says. "If I want to have sex with a girl and she wants to with me, why is it so wrong? It's really our own business."

Yes, you get to choose whether or not to become sexually active. But God says don't. Surprisingly enough, people today are learning that even God's rules about sexual involvement outside of marriage were given because He loves us enough to want the best for our lives.

For the past few decades, people have become more and more open about indulging their sexual desires. Today, live-in arrangements, casual sex, and multiple partners are quite the common thing. The world has adopted an accepting attitude of such practices, and for a few years there did not seem to be any significant societal problems as the result of "the new morality."

Then slowly but surely people began to discover the flaws in the new "freedoms": STDs, unwanted pregnancies, and unimaginable heartache.

A bestselling erotic novel was published and quickly publicized as the most honest piece of writing in years. It told the story of a promiscuous young woman and her many affairs. Erotic? Perhaps. But the underlying theme of the book was that as she lived out her fantasies, they weren't what she really wanted! Her deepest desire was to have a one-to-one relationship with one man—her husband.

A noted psychologist who had been one of six adults to form a commune found himself puzzled after a few months. The group had spent weeks discussing how they wanted to organize their "family." The list of rules and contingencies was quite long. Sexual involvement between members was to be allowed, but only on a one-person-at-a-time basis. Only when one sexual relationship had been terminated could a new one be developed. "If carefully controlled sexual variety is what we all wanted, why does it hurt so much when 'my girl' breaks off with me to sleep with another guy?" he asked.

A few years ago *Cosmopolitan* magazine ran several articles on the hazards couples face when living together without having been married. After a lengthy article about a couple's experiences while living in a commune, the editors of another contemporary magazine that advocates sexual freedom stated that this particular couple had been lucky their marriage survived. Most couples who enter communal living tend to split up because of the experience. This couple had chosen to get an apartment of their own, breaking all ties with members of the commune.

Many non-Christian psychologists take a positive stand on marriage. Because the intimacy of a sexual relationship leads to an emotional attachment, with or without a legal bond, a broken relationship can hurt as much as a broken marriage.

How interesting to discover that when people choose to disobey God's laws about sex, they later discover that His rules were only based on His love for us.

WHAT DOES GOD SAY?

God's principles for moral purity are clearly outlined in His Word.

He designed the human body, including our sexual desires and functions (see Ps. 139:13–17).

Sexual intimacy is to be a part of the husband-wife relationship. Hebrews 13:4 reads, "Let marriage be held in honor among all, and let the marriage bed be undefiled; for fornicators and adulterers God will judge" (NASB; see also Gen. 1:26–31 and 1 Cor. 7:1–5).

Sexual intimacy outside of marriage is expressly forbidden. In fact, the Scriptures teach that those who continue to practice such things are excluded from the kingdom of God (see 1 Cor. 5:9–13; 6:13–20; Eph. 5:3; 1 Thess. 4:3).

We are to resist the temptation to give in to our fleshly lusts.

The promise of 1 Corinthians 10:13 applies even to sexual temptation. "No temptation has overtaken you but such as is common to man; and God is faithful, who will not allow you to be tempted beyond what you are able, but with the temptation will provide the way of escape also, that you may be able to endure it" (NASB; see also Gal. 5:16–21; 1 Peter 2:11–12).

OBEDIENCE IS A DAILY CHOICE

Obedience is a choice we make each time we are tempted to yield to our desire for sexual intimacy outside marriage. If you choose to keep your relationship morally pure, you will want to establish some guidelines to help keep the relationship under control. Helpful ideas include the following:

- Agree to limit your time alone together.
- Plan dates in advance rather than just getting together and doing whatever "feels good."
- Spend more time being actively involved in projects or activities rather than just being together for hours at a time.
- Refrain from behaviors that sexually arouse your partner.
- Avoid external sexual stimuli such as watching sensual movies or dressing seductively.
- Refuse to set the stage for sexual involvement. For example, being alone in one or the other's apartment with mood music, dim lighting, and a romantic fire.

- Be open with each other about the behaviors and situations that make sexual temptation the most difficult to resist and support one another by avoiding those situations.

Learning to live out your commitment to obedience is a major step in your spiritual growth. When you learn how to exercise self-control in sexual matters, you can use the same techniques to master anger, language, and other tendencies to excess. Since the rules were made because of God's love for you, you will find that you are that much more free to live the abundant life when you follow the rules.

As the psalmist says, "Take delight in the LORD and he will give you the desires of your heart. Commit your way to the LORD; trust in him; and he will act" (Ps. 37:4–5 NIV).

10

THE PERFECT ENDING

As the organist hit the opening chords of "The Wedding March" and the wedding guests rose and turned to watch Kathleen walk down the aisle, the minister smiled proudly. If ever a couple had a chance of making their marriage a success, Kathleen and Jonathan were that couple! They had listened to his advise, made wise choices while they were dating, and really worked at developing their relationship. They were ready for this marriage and their life together.

YOU CAN BE READY TOO!

If you and your partner follow the guidelines in this book seriously, you will probably develop a very strong, intimate relationship. Let's review some of the major concepts discussed.

1. Strengthening your self-concepts by accepting the fact that you both have faults as well as virtues allows you to appreciate one another and verbally recognize one another's individual growth and development. Accepting who you are as God's creation allows you to be open and vulnerable with your partner.

2. Understanding the differences and similarities between your approaches to life allows you to anticipate and work through your problems.

3. Clarifying your expectations of yourselves, each other, and the relationship gives you a chance to discard unrealistic fantasies and to help fulfill one another's needs.

4. Choosing and working toward goals in your relationship will bring the two of you closer together because you are investing in one another's lives.

5. Communicating openly and confronting one another in a loving manner builds the trust level as well as the degree of intimacy in your partnership.

6. Spending your time apart from one another in a constructive manner encourages a healthy level of independence in each individual so that while there is a certain amount of interdependence in the relationship, the partners are not wholly dependent upon one another for everything.

7. Seeing one another in a variety of situations over a period of several months helps you get to know your partner.

8. Controlling the progression of the relationship allows the romantic fantasy to evaporate so that the relationship can be built on reality.

9. Limiting the amount of time spent alone together is an exercise in patience and discipline that will be helpful in the course of any long-term relationship.

10. Seeking counseling as a couple can help you anticipate and overcome most major hurdles you may encounter.

If you have taken these steps, you probably have developed a solid friendship, a level of deep emotional intimacy, and a godly physical expression of your love for one another. You will have

FIGURE 10-1

The Complete Talley-Graph Interpersonal Relationship Development Model

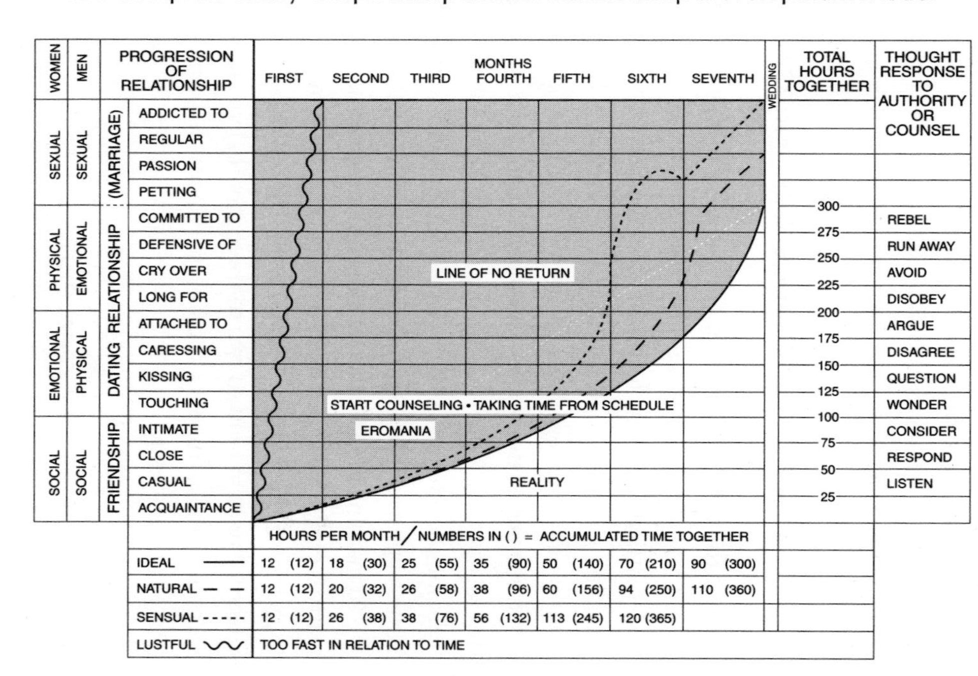

shared on social, recreational, intellectual, and spiritual levels. You will have come to a place of genuine commitment to one another for a lifelong relationship.

This is the type of relationship illustrated by the "ideal" curve in Figure 10-1. It is an ideal foundation on which to build a strong Christian marriage.

WHAT IF WE CHANGE OUR MINDS?

One of the possibilities in any relationship is that one or both of you may change your minds! If the decision is to delay getting married, you can level off the number of hours you are spending together each month and maintain a healthy relationship at its current level for an indefinite period of time.

If the decision is not to get married at all, then you can back the relationship down to the friendship level by significantly reducing the amount of time spent alone together and withdrawing from physical and emotional intimacies that have developed.

Remaining friends is sometimes difficult if the decision not to marry is one-sided. A time of complete separation may be needed to get past the pain of rejection or the awkwardness of the change. But soon (within two to three months) you may want to reconnect and salvage the friendship. Friends are much too valuable to discard easily!

THE END?

Whether the next step is marriage or a return to the friendship level, it is not actually the end of the relationship. Rather, it is just the beginning of a whole new experience in relating.

If you decide to remain friends, then you have developed a bond that is probably stronger than any others you have. How exciting to have such a good friend of the opposite sex to share with, care for, and be loved by. As true brothers and sisters in Christ, you can encourage one another in your Christian walk and provide the full range of male/female perspectives to issues and experiences you each face.

If you do decide to get married, you will have learned a valuable lesson about how to keep your marriage strong. You see, if you start backward on the Talley-Graph Model, moving from right to left and top to bottom, you could plot the death of a marriage. Just as spending time alone together intensifies the development of a relationship, failing to take time to be alone together after marriage will weaken the relationship. At the same time, a decrease in sexual, physical, or emotional sharing will take away from the level of intimacy experienced in the marriage.

So, should you and your partner decide to marry, make a commitment to one another to give high priority to your relationship. You will want to continue to spend quality time alone, sharing your experiences, thoughts, ideas, and feelings.

If both of you do make this commitment, you can discover that your relationship has the strength to survive the inevitable tough times. The tragedy is that sometimes one partner fails to keep the commitment and gives up on the relationship when problems arise. A *daily* renewal of your commitment to God and to one another is the best way to build a lasting Christian family. It's a challenge—and a blessing!

STUDY GUIDE

PART ONE: BEFORE YOU BEGIN

WHAT IS "RELATIONSHIP DISCUSSION"?

Relationship discussion is not premarital counseling. Rather, it is designed to help you learn how to build a relationship *before* you seriously consider a lifelong commitment. By helping you better know yourself and your partner, it will help you to avoid an unstable marriage. If you decide to marry, it is vital that you also go through premarital counseling before you marry.

Almost everyone desires to have a meaningful and fulfilling relationship that will lead to marriage. If you doubt this statement, simply test it by asking a group of single friends, "How many of you are committed to staying single for the rest of your lives?" The answer is almost none! However, the expectation that a dating relationship will automatically lead to marriage can destroy a friendship.

Many people are so determined to get married that they skip

over building a strong relationship upon which a solid marriage can be built. Consequently, thousands are experiencing the pain of broken relationships and divorce.

If used as intended, this material will provide an environment in which a meaningful relationship can develop and will minimize situations and circumstances that can be destructive to a new relationship. The prerequisites on pages 129–32 are an important factor in the effectiveness of this material.

HOW CAN I USE THIS GUIDE?

The eight sessions of relationship discussion are scheduled for every other week, thus giving you one full week to read the material and the following week for you and your partner to meet for discussion. The effectiveness of this program will depend upon how honestly and thoroughly you discuss the material. This guided discussion is the real power force in molding a quality relationship.

Meeting every other week gives you ample time to read and think about the topics that are assigned. If you move at a faster pace, you eliminate the opportunity for the material to penetrate the relationship and produce positive results. Stretching the time needed to complete the workbook over a four-month time period is vital to the process of integration, evaluation, growth, and emotional adjustment.

Most emotionally devastating relationships can be prevented if two people who like each other will give themselves time to become friends. If this material is used properly, you will find that even if your relationship as a serious dating couple ends, you can remain good friends. This is helpful not only to you and your companion but also to your mutual friends. A relationship that ends explosively affects everyone. Let me reemphasize that relationship discussion as presented in this study guide is not intended to take the place of premarital counseling. It can, however, provide a stable basis of evaluation upon which a couple can decide if they want to continue the relationship. In addition to relationship discussion, the author has a four-month workbook program that covers these areas and uses an instructor. This would be pre-premarital, to be used prior to engagement. At the point of engagement, premarital counseling is vital. An engaged couple will view many of the topics covered in this guide in a different light, and additional topics, such as the sexual relationship and dealing with in-laws, must be discussed before marriage. You will benefit greatly from going through relationship discussion, relationship instruction, and premarital counseling as your relationship progresses.

HOW DO I GET STARTED?

The initial steps are very easy. You both must read the prerequisites, sign the written commitment form, and set up your first appointment in two weeks. Then meet every other week and follow the discussion agenda for each of the eight sessions!

INTRODUCTORY SESSION

PREREQUISITES

1. You and your partner must have a strong, consistent friendship with the freedom to hold each other physically.

2. You must be willing to meet for eight sessions, which will

be scheduled every other week for approximately four months. The commitment is to the eight sessions.

3. You must be willing to do one to two hours of reading one week and spend one to two hours the following week discussing the material.

4. No wedding proposal or date should be discussed. If this has already taken place, you both must be willing to put aside wedding plans and be open to the possibility that the relationship may not lead to marriage.

5. Do not talk or even think about marriage between the two of you, even while discussing the word study on marriage. This may be difficult, but it is vital in order to protect the relationship from unrealistic expectations.

6. Be willing to become mutually exclusive, having no relational one-on-one time with anyone else of the opposite sex. This means no luncheon dates, gifts, or romantic personal notes to anyone other than the person going through this with you. If there is another relationship, you must be willing to tell the other person about this four-month commitment. Relationships with members of the opposite sex must be kept at the professional or friendship level.

7. All subjects and discussions are to be confidential to protect the integrity of the relationship.

8. Even if the dating relationship does not continue, the commitment to relationship discussion must continue for the eight sessions. This is to prevent either of you from getting hurt and to test your commitment level.

9. Agree to keep the following limits on time spent together:

First month: 20 hours

Second month: 30 hours

Third month: 40 hours

Fourth month: 50 hours

Time alone is counted hour for hour; group time is divided by four; phone time is counted when the conversation runs over a half hour. Time together is to be recorded on monthly time charts. The total should not exceed 140 hours in the four months.

10. Be honest about the physical part of the relationship. Circle the number that represents the extent of your physical involvement.

1 Look

2 Touch

3 Lightly holding hands

4 Constantly holding hands

5 Light kiss

6 Strong kiss

7 French kiss

8 Fondling breasts

9 Fondling sexual organs

10 Sexual intercourse

11. Make a commitment to keep the physical level at number 7 or below. This is to protect the relationship from being destroyed by excessive physical involvement.

12. If the physical level exceeds number 7, you both must be willing to fill out the Moral Freedom Worksheet in this section. The guy must be willing to contact a pastor or spiritual mentor within twenty-four hours after exceeding the physical limits. If he does not do this, the woman should do so. Letting the pastor know is one way to protect the spiritual lives of both partners as well as the relationship.

13. In the event of a second involvement above number 7, fill out the Moral Purity Worksheet and contact your pastor or a spiritual mentor who can hold you accountable to your commitment to keep the physical involvement at number 7 or below. You should shift to relationship instruction at this point and involve a third party, or the relationship and your spiritual lives will be put in jeopardy (see James 5:16).

WRITTEN COMMITMENT

If you and your partner are both willing to accept the prerequisites and to commit yourselves to relationship discussion, sign and date below.

Signed________________________Dated______________

Signed________________________Dated______________

In the course of this material if you are totally unable to go on, do this word study and give a copy to your partner. Be aware that this is a very serious breach of commitment.

WORD STUDY: *VOW*

1. Dictionary definition of a vow:

2. Write out the following verses in your own words.

   Ecclesiastes 5:4–5

   Numbers 30:2

   Deuteronomy 23:21–23

3. List your reasons for wanting out of this commitment:

GUIDELINES FOR MONTHLY TIME CHARTS

The purpose of the time charts is to provide you with a useful way to keep track of the amount of time you spent together each month. By putting some limits on time spent together, you will appreciate being together more than if you overdo it. Also, physical involvement tends to rise proportionately to the accumulated time together.

The two of you should begin keeping the chart after you both sign the written commitment. The date of the next day should be entered in the first upper-left-hand space; below that, enter the day of the week. Continue likewise throughout the month. Follow the example on the right side of the chart.

ONE-ON-ONE TIME

This includes your discussion times when you are alone together, whether in public or private. Even if other people are around, you are alone unless you are interacting with them. If you just focus on each other while in a group, it's one-on-one time. One-on-one time includes movies, dinners, picnics, and long drives.

GROUP TIME

Consider times when the two of you are interacting with others, such as on double dates, at church, or when working in a group, as group time. The key word is *interacting*. Speaking to the couple at the next table during dinner is not interacting.

PHONE TIME

More than thirty minutes on the phone together is recorded as one-on-one time because of the impact that long, in-depth discussions have on a relationship. Fewer than thirty minutes is not recorded; such contact is helpful to relationships and is encouraged.

The time charts are just one of many tools you will find in this material, but their effectiveness is determined by how completely and honestly they are maintained. They should be reviewed together on a regular basis, and you should both agree on how time together is counted. Also note the shaded section after 2:00 A.M. If you need to be together after these hours, it is important that you be in a group setting or a public environment. This helps to avoid the appearance of evil (see 1 Thess. 5:22).

MONTHLY TIME CHART

HIS NAME ______________ MONTH ______________ GOAL ______________ HER NAME ______________

CALENDAR DATE DAY OF WEEK	1	2	3	4	5	6	7	8	9	10	11	12	13	14	15	16	17	18	19	20	21	22	23	24	25	26	27	28	29	30	31
6																															
7																															
AM 8																															
9																															
10																															
11																															
NOON 12																															
1																															
2																															
3																															
4																															
5																															
PM 6																															
7																															
8																															
9																															
10																															
11																															
MIDNIGHT 12																															
1																															
2																															
AM 3																															
4																															
5																															
SUB-TOTALS																															
ONE-ON-ONE																															
GROUP																															
INTERNET/PHONE																															

x ONE-ON-ONE
o GROUP
· PHONE/INTERNET (OVER 1/2 HOUR)

EXAMPLE

DATE	1	2	3	4	5
DAY	M	T	W	T	F
6	x		·	o	·
7	x		·	o	·
8	o	x	x	o	·
AM 9	o	x	x	o	x
10	·	x	x	·	o
ONE-ON-ONE	2	2	3	0	1
GROUP	2	0	0	4	1
INTERNET/PHONE	1	1	2	1	3

TOTAL HOURS

ONE-ON-ONE ______
GROUP ÷ 4 = ______
PHONE/INTERNET ______

______

MONTHLY TOTAL ______
PREVIOUS TOTAL ______
NEW TOTAL ______

MONTHLY
______
______
______

MONTHLY TIME CHART

HIS NAME ______________ MONTH ______________ GOAL ______________ HER NAME ______________

CALENDAR DATE	1	2	3	4	5	6	7	8	9	10	11	12	13	14	15	16	17	18	19	20	21	22	23	24	25	26	27	28	29	30	31
DAY OF WEEK																															
6																															
7																															
AM 8																															
9																															
10																															
11																															
NOON 12																															
1																															
2																															
3																															
4																															
5																															
PM 6																															
7																															
8																															
9																															
10																															
11																															
MIDNIGHT 12																															
1																															
2																															
AM 3																															
4																															
5																															
SUB-TOTALS																															
ONE-ON-ONE																															
GROUP																															
INTERNET/PHONE																															

- x ONE-ON-ONE
- o GROUP
- · PHONE/INTERNET (OVER 1/2 HOUR)

EXAMPLE

DATE	1	2	3	4	5
DAY	M	T	W	T	F
6	x		·	o	·
7	x		·	o	·
8	o	x	x	o	·
AM 9	o	x	x	o	x
10	·	x	x	·	o
ONE-ON-ONE	2	2	3	0	1
GROUP	2	0	0	4	1
INTERNET/PHONE	1	1	2	1	3

TOTAL HOURS

ONE-ON-ONE ______
GROUP ÷ 4 = ______
PHONE/INTERNET ______

______

MONTHLY TOTAL ______
PREVIOUS TOTAL ______
NEW TOTAL ______

MONTHLY
______
______
______

MONTHLY TIME CHART

HIS NAME ____________ MONTH ____________ GOAL ____________ HER NAME ____________

CALENDAR DATE DAY OF WEEK	1	2	3	4	5	6	7	8	9	10	11	12	13	14	15	16	17	18	19	20	21	22	23	24	25	26	27	28	29	30	31
6																															
7																															
AM 8																															
9																															
10																															
11																															
NOON 12																															
1																															
2																															
3																															
4																															
5																															
PM 6																															
7																															
8																															
9																															
10																															
11																															
MIDNIGHT 12																															
1																															
2																															
AM 3																															
4																															
5																															
SUB-TOTALS																															
ONE-ON-ONE																															
GROUP																															
INTERNET/PHONE																															

x ONE-ON-ONE
o GROUP
· PHONE/INTERNET (OVER 1/2 HOUR)

EXAMPLE

DATE	1	2	3	4	5
DAY	M	T	W	T	F
6	x		·	o	·
7	x		·	o	·
8	o	x	x	o	·
AM 9	o	x	x	o	x
10	·	x	x	·	o
ONE-ON-ONE	2	2	3	0	1
GROUP	2	0	0	4	1
INTERNET/PHONE	1	1	2	1	3

TOTAL HOURS

ONE-ON-ONE ____________
GROUP ÷ 4 = ____________
PHONE/INTERNET ____________

MONTHLY TOTAL ____________
PREVIOUS TOTAL ____________
NEW TOTAL ____________

MONTHLY
____
____
____

MONTHLY TIME CHART

HIS NAME ______________ MONTH ______________ GOAL ______________ HER NAME ______________

CALENDAR DATE DAY OF WEEK	1	2	3	4	5	6	7	8	9	10	11	12	13	14	15	16	17	18	19	20	21	22	23	24	25	26	27	28	29	30	31
6																															
7																															
AM 8																															
9																															
10																															
11																															
NOON 12																															
1																															
2																															
3																															
4																															
5																															
PM 6																															
7																															
8																															
9																															
10																															
11																															
MIDNIGHT 12																															
1																															
2																															
AM 3																															
4																															
5																															
SUB-TOTALS																															
ONE-ON-ONE																															
GROUP																															
INTERNET/PHONE																															

x ONE-ON-ONE
o GROUP
· PHONE/INTERNET (OVER 1/2 HOUR)

EXAMPLE

DATE	1	2	3	4	5
DAY	M	T	W	T	F
6	x		·	o	·
7	x		·	o	·
8	o	x	x	o	·
AM 9	o	x	x	o	x
10	·	x	x	·	o
ONE-ON-ONE	2	2	3	0	1
GROUP	2	0	0	4	1
INTERNET/PHONE	1	1	2	1	3

TOTAL HOURS

ONE-ON-ONE ______________
GROUP ÷ 4 = ______________
PHONE/INTERNET ______________

____

MONTHLY TOTAL ______________
PREVIOUS TOTAL ______________
NEW TOTAL ______________

MONTHLY
____
____
____

MORAL FREEDOM WORKSHEET

1. Write out 1 Corinthians 10:13 in your own words.

____

____

____

____

2. List any ways of escape from temptation that God provided but that you did not use. Remember that God promises to provide escape.

____

____

____

____

3. What steps could be taken to help prevent recurrence?

____

____

____

____

4. Should you further limit your time alone together?

   Circle one: Yes No

5. Have you confessed your failure to God and also asked forgiveness from the other person?

   Circle one: Yes No

6. List two negative results this involvement has had on the relationship.

____

____

____

____

____

____

____

____

7. What places should be off-limits?

____

____

____

____

8. You should wait six weeks from your last sexual encounter and then be tested for AIDS.

MORAL PURITY WORKSHEET

1. What are the dictionary definitions of:

   Purity

   ___

   ___

   ___

   ___

   Fornication

   ___

   ___

   ___

   ___

2. Read Ephesians 5:1–17. How should we respond to fornication?

   ___

   ___

   ___

   ___

3. Read 1 Thessalonians 4:1–7. What is God's will for us?

   ___

   ___

   ___

   ___

4. Read 1 Corinthians 5:1–8. What should the church do about sexual immorality among its members?

5. Read 1 Corinthians 6:13–20. What should we do?

6. Read James 5:16. Why is it important for us to be honest with others about sin?

7. Am I involved in fornication?

8. What do I need to do?

9. It is important that you be tested for AIDS if you've had sex.

PREPARATION FOR SESSION ONE

ASSIGNMENTS:

Read Chapter 1.

Complete the word study on *love.*

Write your autobiography.

Answer the questions on Chapter 1.

WORD STUDY: *LOVE*

1. Discuss the dictionary definition of *love.*

2. Define these Greek words for *love* (ask a Christian friend or pastor if necessary).

   Phileo (love of friends) ________________________________

   ____

   ____

   ____

   Eros (physical love) ________________________________

   ____

   ____

   ____

   Agape (unconditional love) ____________________________

   ____

   ____

   ____

3. First Corinthians 13 describes love as:

____

____

____

AUTOBIOGRAPHY

Briefly describe the following time periods of your lives:

Childhood

____

____

____

____

Teenage Years

____

____

____

____

College Years

____

____

____

____

Adult Years

____

____

____

____

Describe the kind of person you want to be and what you want to be doing in ten years.

____

____

____

____

____

CHAPTER I QUESTIONS

1. What are the indications that a friendship has progressed to a romance?

____

____

____

____

2. How does today's "disposable society" affect a relationship or friendship?

____

____

____

____

3. List two differences between romance and love from Chapter 1.

____

____

____

____

____

4. Can there be romance (eromania) in a relationship without physical intimacy?

   ____

5. How is such a romance expressed?

   ____

   ____

   ____

   ____

6. How do relationships tend to progress differently for guys and women?

   ____

   ____

   ____

   ____

7. Do something special for each other each week that will express romance without the physical aspect of touch being involved.

PREPARATION FOR SESSION TWO

ASSIGNMENTS:

Read Chapter 2.
Complete the Friendship Evaluation.
Complete the study on commitment.
Answer the questions on Chapter 2.

FRIENDSHIP EVALUATION

1. How did you meet?

____

____

____

2. List one strength, and one weakness of your friendship.

____

____

____

____

____

____

3. How has the time you spend together affected your same-sex friendships?

____

____

____

COMMITMENT STUDY

1. Respond to the following statement: "I am committed to God's best for your life, even if that means I cannot be a part of it." Can you say this to your partner honestly?

   ____

2. List three actions that indicate commitment:

   By him, toward her:

   ____

   ____

   ____

   By her, toward him:

   ____

   ____

   ____

3. List three actions that indicate a lack of commitment:

   By him, toward her:

   ____

   ____

   ____

   By her, toward him:

   ____

   ____

   ____

4. In your opinion, what is the most vital sign of commitment?

   ____

   ____

5. How would you describe trust?

____

____

____

____

CHAPTER 2 QUESTIONS

1. In one sentence summarize the principle of the Talley-Graph.

____

____

____

2. Give a personal example of the principle.

____

____

____

____

3. What attracted you to this relationship? What were you looking for?

____

____

____

____

____

4. What would you say the other person was attracted to?

____

____

____

____

5. "Too many consecutive hours spent _______together can ____________ resistance to ______________________." (See page 29)

6. According to pages 25–26, what are two advantages to not being sexually active before marriage?

____
____
____

____
____
____

SESSION TWO

TIME: FRIEND OR FOE?

DISCUSSION AGENDA

1. Pray together for God's direction during this meeting and for each other in general.

2. Discuss how you view your friendship. You do not have to agree on everything. As the saying goes, "If you both agree on everything, one of you is not necessary." The key is to understand each other's viewpoint, not necessarily to change it.

3. Review how you met.

4. Review Chapter 2, and note any differences in your answers to the questions based on that chapter. Discuss them thoroughly.

5. Take time to discuss each other's answers to the commitment study. Be honest as you share your feelings, and listen carefully to each other. This is a good time to check how well you are communicating by using the phrase, "Let me be sure I understand . . ." and then repeating what the other person just said. Let him/her respond to your conclusions.

6. Have you exceeded number 7 on the physical involvement list?

   ____

7. Review the monthly time chart, and use it to evaluate where and when you spend your time together. Are you avoiding the appearance of evil (see 1 Thess. 5:22)? Look at things from your neighbor's perspective. Discuss the relationship between long periods of time alone together and increased physical involvement.

8. State one positive thing you have learned about the other person.

   ____

   ____

   ____

   ____

9. Review your next assignments, and close in prayer.

PREPARATION FOR SESSION THREE

ASSIGNMENTS:

Read Chapters 3 and 4.

Respond to the questions on aloneness.

Answer the questions based on Chapters 3 and 4.

ALONENESS

1. List two positives of living alone.

___

___

___

___

2. List two positives of living with a same-sex roommate.

___

___

___

___

3. If Adam were created perfect and sinless prior to the Fall, why was he lonely?

___

___

___

4. Respond to the statement, "You are not ready for a relationship until you are content to be alone."

____

CHAPTER 3 QUESTIONS

1. According to James Fairfield, what are two responses to conflict (see pages 43–44)?

____

____

____

____

____

____

2. Which response do you use when you have a conflict?

____

3. Tell about a recent and rewarding incident when both of you used "resolve" to solve a conflict with the guidance of the Holy Spirit.

4. "Sharing spiritually has the greatest impact on the quality and depth of a relationship" (see page 46). Discuss this statement.

5. Guys: Do you see yourself leading and encouraging her in the spiritual matters of your relationship?

   Girls: Do you find it difficult to follow him in spiritual matters?

6. Where would you rate yourself spiritually today?

   Poor Average Good Excellent

CHAPTER 4 QUESTIONS

1. "People are not ready to marry until they are content to be single." Do you agree?

   ____

   ____

2. Would you say you were content in your single life before you began this relationship?

   ____

   ____

3. In your opinion, when is a person ready for a relationship with the opposite sex?

   ____

   ____

YOUR SPIRITUAL LIFE

4. Is your quiet time with the Lord better or worse since you began this relationship?

   ____

   ____

YOUR SOCIAL LIFE

5. Has your dating affected your close and intimate same-sex friendships?

   ____

   ____

SESSION THREE

TOGETHERNESS IS NOT ENOUGH!

DISCUSSION AGENDA

1. Woman: Open with prayer, asking God to help both of you visualize the plan He has for your lives.

2. Review the issue of aloneness, and discuss the positives of living alone and of same-sex roommates. Share who your best same-sex friend is and how long you have been friends.

3. Compare your answers for Chapters 3 and 4. Have you been able to develop the conflict-resolving skills that are needed for a quality relationship? Are you able to relate to each other on a spiritual level?

4. Go over the monthly time chart together. Be sure it is current and that you both agree on how the time is being recorded.

5. Pray and thank God for one special quality in your partner's life.

PREPARATION FOR SESSION FOUR

ASSIGNMENTS:

Read Chapters 5 and 6.

Respond to the questions about self-improvement.

Respond to the questions on Chapters 5 and 6.

SELF-IMPROVEMENT

1. What two changes do you believe God wants to make in your life?

2. What two changes do you believe God wants to make in your partner's life?

CHAPTER 5 QUESTIONS

1. Why is a positive self-image important to the dating relationship?

   ____

   ____

   ____

   ____

2. How would you describe your self-image?

   Poor   Average   Good   Excellent

3. Discuss what actions or behaviors show that a person has a low self-esteem.

4. Read Psalm 139:1–6 and discuss the passage with your partner.

CHAPTER 6 QUESTIONS

1. Why do you think it is important to discuss the differences between men and women?

   ____

   ____

   ____

   ____

2. Girls: Read 1 Timothy 3:1–13 and review the qualities of a godly man.

3. Guys: Read Proverbs 31:10–31 and review the characteristics of a virtuous woman.

4. Discuss your expectations of an ideal partner.

   Spiritual

   Financial

   Physical

   Emotional

   Other

SESSION FOUR

ONE OF A KIND

DISCUSSION AGENDA

1. Man: Pray that both you and your partner will be open to the will of God.

2. Share with each other the two changes God wants to make in your lives. Compare individually what you feel God wants you to change in your life.

3. Discuss the chapters on self-esteem and the differences between men and women.

4. Have you exceeded number 7 on the physical involvement list? If the answer is no, encourage each other, and continue to monitor your time together. If yes, refer to the Moral Freedom Worksheet (p. 140).

5. State how you think the other person is doing in regard to relationship discussion in general and your relationship in

particular. Discuss and evaluate any changes in your commitment to each other. Is it increasing, maintaining, or declining?

6. Pray aloud for changes your partner feels God wants to make in his/her life.

PREPARATION FOR SESSION FIVE

ASSIGNMENTS:

Read Chapter 7.

Respond to the questions about finances.

Respond to the questions on Chapter 7.

Finances

1. Was your checkbook balanced to the penny last month?

____

2. Circle your approximate net worth in thousands:
   $0–25 $25–75 $75–100 $100–150+

3. How much debt do you owe and for what?

____

____

____

____

____

____

4. Have you refinanced your house or other bills in the last year?

____

5. Have you ever been in bankruptcy?

6. Do you have a savings account over $500?

7. Do you have a retirement fund?

8. Are you in debt to any relatives?

9. Do you tithe on your net or gross income? Or neither?

10. Do you expect your mate, if you marry, to combine financial resources with you?

11. How do you see the finances being handled best in a marriage?

12. What are your short-term, mid-range, and long-range financial goals?

    Short-term

    ____

    ____

    ____

    Mid-range

    ____

    ____

    ____

    Long-range

    ____

    ____

    ____

SPIRITUAL EVALUATION

1. Discuss how you became a Christian.

2. Highlight your spiritual growth pattern for the last five years.

3. Evaluate your spiritual growth in each area by placing the appropriate number in the blank.

   1 Poor 2 Average 3 Good 4 Excellent

   ____Quiet time
   ____Prayer
   ____Scripture memory
   ____Witnessing
   ____Control of bad habits
   ____Stewardship (tithe)
   ____Church attendance
   ____Bible study
   ____Accountability

CHAPTER 7 QUESTIONS

1. Share a personal experience when one of your unrealistic expectations had an adverse effect on the relationship.

2. Discuss one cherished unmet expectation in this relationship.

3. What steps do you think are needed to correct unrealistic expectations in a relationship?

____

____

____

____

SESSION FIVE

FAIRY TALES OR REALITY?

DISCUSSION AGENDA

1. Open your session in prayer.

2. Discuss any conflicts that may have arisen so far in your relationship. Are you able to understand each other's viewpoints and resolve differences?

3. As you review the answers under "Finances," be aware that disagreements in this area are a major cause of divorce. Do this discussion in depth.

4. Discuss in detail any unrealistic expectations you have identified in yourself. Be honest, and share how you are dealing with unfulfilled expectations.

5. Compare your differences on the spiritual evaluation. In what areas do you need to grow? How can you help each other?

6. By now the material should be drawing the two of you into deeper involvement. This will increase the tension in some areas of the relationship, but learning to handle the tension is important in the development of a strong and enduring relationship. No pain, no gain.

7. Pray for each other's spiritual life.

PREPARATION FOR SESSION SIX

ASSIGNMENTS:

Read Chapter 8.

Complete the word study on *marriage.*

Respond to the questions on Chapter 8.

WORD STUDY–*MARRIAGE*

1. Discuss three things you see in your relationship with your partner that are obstacles to overcome in order to have a successful marriage.
2. Discuss three things you see in your relationship with your partner that would contribute to a successful marriage.
3. Have you ever been involved in a pregnancy?

   ____

4. Have you been married?

   a. Are you scripturally free to remarry?

   ____

   b. Why? Discuss Matthew 19:9; Matthew 5:32; 1 Corinthians 7:10–11; Deuteronomy 24:4.

   ____

   ____

   ____

   ____

CHAPTER 8 QUESTIONS

1. What role do goals play in your life?

2. In your opinion, why do you need to set goals?

3. Give the authors' reasons for setting goals (see pages 96–97).

4. What role do goals play in a relationship?

5. Discuss the characteristics of good goals (see pages 99–101).

PREPARATION FOR SESSION SEVEN

ASSIGNMENTS:

Read Chapter 9.

Respond to the questions about children.

Respond to the questions on Chapter 9.

CHILDREN

1. Do you want children?

    ___

2. Do you have any children?

    ___

3. If you both had custody of all your children under the age of eighteen, how many children would you have?

    ___

4. If you married a person with children, would you be willing for the children to live with you?

    ___

5. Do you believe in corporal punishment (spanking)?

    ___

    How do you think children should be disciplined?

    ___

    ___

    ___

Who do you think should be the primary disciplinarian in the family?

____

CHAPTER 9 QUESTIONS

1. What does God say about sexual temptation in the following verses?

   1 Corinthians 6:13–20

   ____

   ____

   ____

   1 Peter 2:11–12

   ____

   ____

   ____

2. Why do people often rush into commitment in a relationship?

   ____

   ____

   ____

3. List two problems with allowing a relationship to break up.

   ____

   ____

   ____

4. What do you think causes a relationship to break up?

____

____

____

5. What do you do when you are faced with sexual temptation in your relationship?

____

____

____

session seven

AVOIDING THE PITFALLS

DISCUSSION AGENDA

1. Open in prayer for God's wisdom.
2. Review the issue of children. Be honest—this is one of the major causes of divorce!
3. Discuss your answers to the Chapter 9 questions. Review how each of you views the relationship up to this point. Is the relationship improving and deepening or moving back toward friendship?
4. Evaluate the monthly time chart. Do you need to make any changes in when, where, or how much time you are spending together?
5. Close in prayer.

PREPARATION FOR SESSION SEVEN

ASSIGNMENTS:

Read Chapter 10.
Respond to the questions on Chapter 10.
Consider what direction your relationship might take after completing this next session. Be prepared to share your choice for the relationship with your partner.

CHAPTER 10 QUESTIONS

1. Without referring to the book, discuss three principles that have influenced you.

2. Share a positive impact one of these principles has had on your relationship:

____

____

____

____

3. What options are open to a couple who decides not to get married after having had a serious dating relationship?

____

____

____

____

4. Evaluate your stability in the following area.
   1 Poor 2 Average 3 Good 4 Excellent

   ____Mentally
   ____Emotionally
   ____Physically
   ____Relationally
   ____Financially

5. List two objections your parents might have if you decide to marry in six months.

   ____
   ____
   ____

   ____
   ____
   ____

6. If you followed your parents' advice, would you marry this person?

   ____

7. If you have been married before, did your parents approve?

   ____

POSSIBLE NEW DIRECTIONS

Your commitment not to talk or think about marriage with each other is now completed. You need to discuss your honest responses to each of the options below for your future direction together. Where do we go from here? Be *honest!*

1. Go back to friendship:

    Pro ______________________________

    Con ______________________________

2. Go on to relationship instructions:

    Pro ______________________________

    Con ______________________________

3. Consider reconciliation with former spouse:

    Pro ______________________________

    Con ______________________________

4. Discuss marriage:

    Pro ______________________________

    Con ______________________________

SESSION EIGHT

THE PERFECT ENDING

DISCUSSION AGENDA

1. Pray together and thank God for one specific thing you have learned about yourself over the past four months.

2. Discuss the Chapter 10 questions. Concentrate on how important it is to have your parents' support of your relationship.

3. Review the pros and cons of each choice for a new direction. Determine the new direction for you as a couple. Remember that the relationship is controlled by the person who is least sure of his/her commitment.

4. Have you exceeded number 7 on the physical involvement list? If the answer is no, encourage one another. If you have not been past number 7 since the program began, you are to be commended. Approximately 70 percent of the couples the author has counseled have had problems in this area. It would be good to review the verses on the Moral Purity Sheet.

5. If you have had trouble controlling the physical dimension of the relationship, or if you plan to marry, you should see your pastor or counselor within one week.

6. If one or both of you are hurting emotionally because of the new direction you or your partner has decided to take, I recommend you read *Quality Friendships* by Gary Inrig and review the friendship agreement on pages 37–38.

7. Pray for one another! You survived the Talley-Graph.

OUR DIRECTION

His direction is

____

____

____

____

____

Her direction is

____

____

____

____

____

Together we have decided to

____

____

____

____

____

EVALUATION

1. What was the most beneficial part of relationship discussion for you?

   ____

   ____

2. What material or session was the least helpful?

   ____

   ____

3. What changes would you make in your relationship if you could do it over?

   ____

   ____

4. Give two examples of how this material has affected your life.

   ____

   ____

   ____

   ____

5. Would you recommend this book to others?

   ____

Please send your evaluation and/or comments to Dr. Jim A. Talley.

Relationship Resources, Inc.
11805 Sylvester Dr.
Oklahoma City, Oklahoma 73162-1018
phone: (405) 720-8300
e-mail: *drtalley@drtalley.com*

ALSO BY DR. JIM A. TALLEY

Reconcilable Differences

In the course of counseling since 1970 and building an extensive single adult ministry, Dr. Talley has discovered that many of the separated and divorced couples he counsels are open to the idea of reconciliation. They may be hostile and even bitter toward their spouses, but they truly desire a lessening of tension and a return to friendly relations—especially if children are involved.

Reconcilable Differences shows why it is worth the effort for troubled couples to try again and, more important, how it can be done. It describes individual situations where love was rekindled and gives specific guidelines for overcoming the differences in a marriage that cause alienation and lead to separation. *Reconcilable Differences* gives invaluable suggestions to any couple—married, separated, or divorced—for rebuilding their relationship and developing a foundation based on mutual love, respect, and trust.

Reconciliation Instruction is a four-month workbook program designed to reconcile troubled marriages, separated couples, or couples that are divorced where neither has remarried.

Relationship Instruction. The study guide used in this book is an outline of a more comprehensive, four-month workbook program titled *Relationship Instruction.* This is a powerful program, designed to strengthen intimacy and increase commitment before marriage. If you would like to order this program or any other of Dr. Talley's resources, you may contact him at:

Relationship Resources, Inc.
11805 Sylvester Dr.
Oklahoma City, Oklahoma 73162-1018
phone: (405) 720-8300
e-mail: *drtalley@drtalley.com*
www.drtalley.com

ABOUT THE AUTHORS

DR. JIM A. TALLEY has been involved in counseling since 1970. He has experience in teaching and developing innovative single adult ministries, including Relationship Resources, a ministry focused on the strengthening, renewing, and reconciliation of marriages. As a national speaker and author of six books, Dr. Talley has appeared on numerous television and radio programs. He is the former director of the National Singles Conference. He and his wife, Joyce, live in Oklahoma City, Oklahoma, where he is a licensed marriage and family therapist in private practice. For more information on Dr. Talley, visit www.drtalley.com.

DR. BOBBIE REED has doctorates in social psychology and ministry, with an emphasis in single adult ministry. She has authored thirty-seven books on relationships, personal growth, Christian education, parenting, and successful living as a single adult. For the past twenty-eight years she has been a conference speaker and a consultant on single adult ministry across the United States. She and her husband, Ed, live in San Diego, California.